CYBERSECURITY SURVIVAL STRATEGIES

TIPS FOR LOCAL AND GLOBAL CYBERSECURITY

NICK SELBY AND HEATHER VESCENT

Rosen YA
New York

This edition published in 2019 by:
The Rosen Publishing Group, Inc.
29 East 21st Street
New York, NY 10010

Cataloging-in-Publication Data

Names: Selby, Nick. | Vescent, Heather.
Title: Tips for local and global cybersecurity / Nick Selby and Heather Vescent.
Description: New York : Rosen YA, 2019. | Series: Cybersecurity survival strategies
| Includes glossary and index.
Identifiers: ISBN 9781508186410 (library bound)
Subjects: LCSH: Computer crimes—Juvenile literature. | Computer crimes—Prevention—Juvenile literature.
| Computer security—Juvenile literature. | Computer networks—Security measures—Juvenile literature.
Classification: LCC HV6773.S453 2019 | DDC 364.16'8—dc23

Manufactured in the United States of America

CONTENTS

THIS BOOK IS ALREADY OUT OF DATE (AND THAT'S OKAY)

Every day there seems to be a new story about cybercrime: millions of credit cards stolen, private celebrity photos leaked, foreign agents interfering at the highest levels of government. It's hard for even the best-informed reader to know how much of this is real versus scare-mongering clickbait, and how to react regardless. Sadly, many people either become so paralyzed by fear that they vacillate between different strategies for too long/ Conversely, some decide it's all too much and try to ignore the topic completely.

The thing is, each of us is utterly reliant on cybersecurity in ways both obvious and unexpected. As a police officer, I've brusquely knocked on the door of the suspect in a cyber case only to find a 78-year-old retiree, innocent of anything but a yen for some specialized, icky, but legal movies. Our man made a rookie mistake by going for the free icky-but-legal films, unaware of the first rule of the web: if you can't figure out how someone makes money on a site, you're the product. Criminals had planted malware in his naughty movies and were renting cyber scammers remote access to his computer, unbeknownst to him.

Some of the hacks we describe will be old news tomorrow. Some will take on new and more insidious forms. And something new will pop up every time you turn around. That's okay—this book gives you the tools you need to understand what your digital footprint looks like to criminals, advertisers, investigators, and governments, and how to figure out and fix your vulnerabilities even as the specific threats change.

We can't tell you everything that might happen to you—some of next week's threats are being cooked up right now in basements and labs from Missouri to Moldova. But we can tell you how to reduce your risks no matter what. Security experts like to talk about OPSEC (operational security). And OPSEC is OPSEC—today and forever. It's not about specific dangers, it's about a mind-set of preparedness.

Understanding your digital universe and the consequences of your actions will reduce the things that can make you a victim, without your having to miss out everything the internet has to offer. This book will help you better understand the kinds of threats out there, and give you the tools and perspective to protect yourself. The rest is up to you.

NICK SELBY

ALSO, THIS BOOK WILL FREAK YOU OUT (AND THAT'S ALSO OKAY)

To put it simply, you're in danger. Your identity, your bank accounts, and even your government are vulnerable to attack from cyber criminals around the world. That should freak you out. But this book is much more than a collection scary stories (although it's that too). It's also a toolkit for protecting yourself and your data in an increasingly dangerous online world.

The digital age has given us a dazzling array of products and services at our fingertips, but also created new and often unexpected problems. Security technology will continue to get better—and criminals will keep finding new ways to get around that technology. That's where we come in.

How to get your head around security in the modern age? Most people want to know first and foremost how to avoid getting hacked. That's the wrong mindset. It's almost inevitable that you're going to be hacked at some point in your life online.

Start with the assumption that even the most secure technologies are vulnerable. There's an ongoing war between criminal hackers and security experts, and that's not going to change. The only way we can "win" is to assume everything will be hacked, and take precautions to secure what is important. If you expect this inevitable hacking of your security systems, you will be able to understand the risk factors and monitor your security on an ongoing basis. You'll know the places you are vulnerable and be able to take appropriate precautions.

How to know which are the appropriate precautions? That's easy. Read this book! Many of the vulnerabilities enumerated in this book can be dealt with relatively easily, once you have the know-how. You don't need to have the most secure system, just the best one for your needs. Not sure what those are? We'll help you figure that out.

In a sense, hackers are helping us–in their own way. Every time they break a system, we learn something new about its vulnerability, and how to make it more secure. I personally look forward to the new and exciting ways hackers will point out the limitations of each new technology. I just don't want them learning on you!

HEATHER VESCENT

CHAPTER 1

CYBERSECURITY AND YOUR BUSINESS

WHETHER YOU'RE SELLING HANDMADE CRAFTS OUT OF YOUR HOME OR RUNNING A BOOMING ONLINE EMPORIUM, YOU FACE A UNIQUE SET OF RISKS IN THE NEW GLOBAL MARKETPLACE AND NEED TO PROTECT YOURSELF AND YOUR CUSTOMERS.

Starting a business is incredibly risky and incredibly expensive, and keeping one going is rarely much easier. Unexpected costs are everywhere, and it goes without saying that business owners will try to save money wherever they can without sacrificing the quality of their goods. Over and over we see that it's very tempting to scrimp on computer costs.

Before we talk about software licenses and antivirus programs and password strength and monitoring, we need to ask a basic question: What, exactly, qualifies as a business these days? Two of the contributors to this book run businesses from their homes. They have business bank accounts, bookkeepers, and accountants, and they do all their work while sitting in a comfy chair, wearing a pair of bunny slippers. The internet has changed the economy so much from the way it was even in the early 1990s that sometimes Boomers, Gen Xers, and Millennials have vastly different concepts of what constitutes a business.

If you remember what a Beanie Baby is, you remember the turning point in America after which people could actually make a living selling junk on the internet. Today, twenty-five million people make their living in whole or in part by selling things on auction sites.

THIS IS SERIOUS BUSINESS Profit is revenue minus expenses, and one thing home businesses do is generate revenues that are typically much higher than profits. A business phone account can cost twice as much as an ordinary one, for example, and reserving space for a business is yet another overhead cost. There's also the cost of handling utilities and licenses, the expenditures in hiring and training employees if you expand, maintaining the various supplies needed for the business's upkeep, insurance fees, and loss of inventory from accident or theft—and that's to say nothing of the cost of any electronic or internet-based aspects. All these expenses mean that a loss can be devastating to the owner. And when home businesspeople, for example, conduct business on the same poorly protected Wi-Fi network on which their teenagers have access, tragedy is lurking just around the corner.

HOME-BASED BUSINESS BASICS No matter how small your business, safeguarding it is critical. You might ask, "Who would ever target me?" The answer is "criminals." They can attack you with great ease and with efficiency. There is actually a search engine on the internet that does nothing but map the machines that are sitting there connected to the internet—it's called Shodan, and it is just one way that your internet-connected refrigerator is in fact known to hackers and vulnerable to attack. Protect yourself.

BUSINESS SENSE

While most online small-business owners take at least some precautions against cyber attacks, many are still dangerously exposed. Here are some estimates of what risks they're taking.

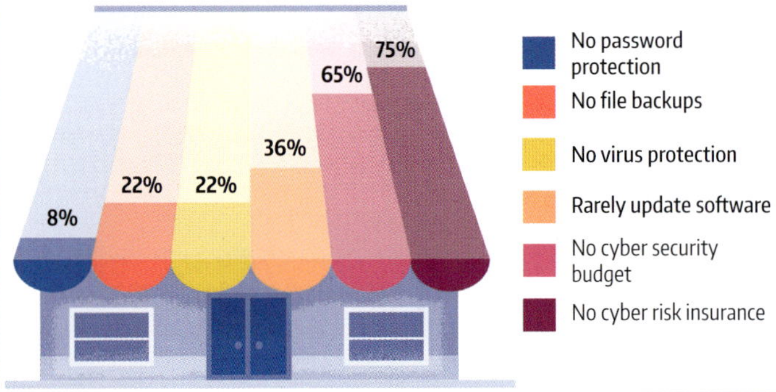

Build a Wall The first thing you will need is a business-grade firewall. This doesn't need to be expensive—you can get a good-quality home-business firewall for about $200 USD. But business firewalls do some things that home firewalls don't do—or at least do them better: opening ports for virtual private networks, examining packets, and providing services that are above the needs of home users.

Stay Connected You'll need a good, solid way to connect to the internet. Cable modem users might find it best to buy their own (I use an ARRIS modem, made by Motorola), as opposed to leasing one from the cable company, because the connection is actually better and a little faster. Also consider a managed DNS service. This allows content filtering for your employees and can keep malware activity to a minimum. You'll need a decent-grade Wi-Fi access point that supports at least WPA2 pre-shared key (PSK) encryption. Use a strong key and rotate it at least semiannually to keep terminated employees off your network when they are no longer employed.

SECURITY BASIC

SET SOME GROUND RULES There are a few prime directives you have to follow in business: Buy low and sell high, always make payroll, and don't make a mess where you expect to eat. In other words, if you're selling merchandise on Facebook or eBay, use a dedicated computer for those transactions, and use it for nothing else.

Imagine that you are a taxi driver. You wouldn't want to use your taxi to drive down to the corner store and get milk and bread, or take it on a trip across town running errands, would you? The taxi would be your business vehicle, and you would use it only for business. The same goes with your digital storefront. Make it exclusive to the business, and only use it for that. This can limit any potential exposure to bad things, especially since this is the primary place you buy ads, sell products, and interact with money.

Let Business Be Business Keeping your work separate from other affairs is about maintaining an atmosphere of professionalism and safety. Do not let your friends or nonbusiness users or traffic on your business network at all. And buy a few hours' help from a local computer outlet—it's worth it to have a checkup on your business network and computer, as well as any necessary maintenance. The silliest thing to come out of the mouths of most smart people is, "I don't have anything worth stealing."

SECURITY BASIC

GROUND RULES FOR SELLING ONLINE Give me your first name, your occupation, and your home city, and I can likely find out almost anything about you in a few searches. Give me your email address, and I can get your Social Security number and full credit file in minutes. And I use legal sites. Imagine what criminals can do.

Even when selling something like a barbecue grill through local ads, be very careful about what information you reveal about yourself. If you're engaging in an online transaction or starting an online dating profile, consider creating a brand-new anonymous email address. Use your first initial only, and be careful about what information you give out. Does Craigslist really need your full address to list a cabinet you're selling? Of course not. Engage in emails with the person you are meeting, and trust your gut about what feels wrong—listen to your instincts, because they are correct.

If you get to the point of a phone call, consider a burner app (available on mobile phones) or a burner phone. Be slow to hand over your number, and agree to meet in public first. Again: Your gut should be in the driver's seat. Make sure someone knows where you are going and with whom you plan to meet—leave a bread-crumb trail in case something bad happens. Consider meeting at a sanctioned online transaction zone set up by local police departments for in-person transactions.

GOOD TO KNOW

DON'T WORK WHERE YOU PLAY When you are working at home, definitely think twice before engaging in any business activities on the same network that your friends are also using to play online multiplayer games at the same time. In fact, you should probably just keep your business traffic out of all other networks, and keep all other traffic out of a business-based network. The best way to do this is through a virtual private network (VPN), which is essentially an encrypted tunnel through which your business traffic is shunted back inside your business firewall and then out onto the internet at large. Another option is a mobile Wi-Fi hot spot that only you are able to use and that you will be using for business and only for business. The advice from the movie *Ghostbusters*—"Don't cross the streams"—should suffice here to keep you out of trouble.

GOOD TO KNOW

IMPROVE YOUR INSURANCE You shouldn't assume that your homeowner's or renter's policy will cover you and all of your equipment that's related to your small business—quite often it won't, if you are genuinely running a business from home. And it obviously won't cover your data losses, no matter what. You'll need some type of special business-related insurance rider to cover all the good stuff.

You'll also do well to get your business set up with surveillance cameras that can store video in the cloud (off-site) and that will allow you to view the videos remotely. Should you ever happen to become burglarized (or vandalized or worse), the first question the cops will ask you is, "Do you happen to have any surveillance video?" If you are able to answer their question with a yes, they will become noticeably more interested in their work.

STAY SAFE One exciting way to meet some of the less-scrupulous people in your neighborhood is to install a lot of expensive business equipment in your house. The realities of life in America mean that computer gear provides thieves with tempting targets, but there are steps you should take to protect the most important assets: yourself, your family, your data, and your equipment—in that order.

Don't Advertise You should definitely place your office out of public view, and try to keep the shades drawn and equipment out of sight from outside when you are not around. Invest in an alarm system that has sensors on your windows and doors as well as panic buttons, and the alarm company you choose should monitor the house 24/7/365 and be able to call you or the police at the first sign of trouble. Not only is this great comfort, but it has the benefit of deterring thieves (they see the signs and move to easier prey) and lowering your homeowner's and business insurance costs.

Save the Data Next up is your data. As the veteran of an office that was burglarized by thieves who stole our computers and our backup drive, I heartily recommend cloud-based backup. Don't skimp on a backup solution, especially in an era of ransomware—your backups are what will save your company. Consider turning on Bitlocker for Windows or File Vault for Macs to stop thieves from harvesting data from your stolen goods. This feature for Windows requires the Professional version.

Work with Employees For those who are considering hiring other remote workers, your considerations will be all of the above, plus ensuring you maintain control over shared data. And when you part ways, you'll want to be sure to get your equipment back and "de-provision" them (lock them out of your network and third-party applications).

SORRY BOSS, MY BAD

Employers are put at risk by their staff every day. Here are some of the most common goof-ups that can expose a company to risk.

SMALL BUSINESSES AND HACKERS Larger businesses and corporations may get a lot more visibility in the press when a hack happens, but that doesn't mean criminals aren't targeting small business every day. In fact, smaller businesses occupy a certain sweet spot for cybercrime. That's because they have more information and assets than a singular consumer, while also being unable to afford as much in terms of security as larger companies.

Just like real-world thieves, cybercriminals will happily take everything they can if they break in, including financial information and records that belong not just to you but to any consumer or client registered with your business—and all of those stolen identities can be used elsewhere. Even your business machines can be locked up with ransomware or infected and drawn, zombie-like, into a botnet for other hacking misdeeds.

So, what can you do to protect your business, its data, and your clients from the effects of a data breach? Quite a lot, actually.

Get Insured Aside from the various security measures we've already covered, cybersecurity insurance is an important part of covering all your bases. Make sure that the policies you consider will cover first-party liability (costs from a breach, legal fees, interruption of business, customer notification, and public relations) and third-party liability (to protect you should your company be involved in a breach that exposes sensitive information about others).

Purge Regularly Never retain business data longer than you must. Once data is not needed, or older than, say, a year, delete it all. Credit card numbers are highly regulated: Understand your obligations under the Payment Card Industry Data Security Standard (PCI-DSS).

Stage a Drill Make it a practice to, well, practice your business's response in the event of a breach. Take the time to formulate, review, and (with each drill) update your response plan as necessary. Perform these exercises at least quarterly, look for any errors or holes in your plan, and then fix them.

Prepare for the Worst Should your business end up the victim of a hack, get to work immediately to find out exactly what happened and put a stop to it, whether that means software patches or a complete takedown and cleanup of your system. Restore any damaged software and documents from backups. Contact your insurer, and get legal advice if you must. Inform your clients as soon as possible of the breach and its nature as it relates to them.

SECURITY BASIC

BACK IT UP Be rigorous about backing up data and storing it in separate places. The best bet is to store things locally, as well as in the cloud. Small businesses can use commercial cloud solutions like Dropbox, SpiderOak, or Backblaze (about $100 USD for two years with unlimited data). Augment this with daily (or more frequent) snapshots of your environment stored elsewhere. A good rule to remember for your business backups is 3-2-1: at least three total copies of your data, two of which are local but on different media (maybe a USB drive or a network-attached storage device) and at least one copy off-site. And be aware the backing up is just your first step. At some point, you will want to test to see if you can restore files. Businesses have thought that they were backing up data only to have some level of corruption ultimately invalidate all the hard work they'd put in.

NEVER CHEAP OUT ON BUILDING AN E-COMMERCE SITE. LOOK AT THE MONEY YOU SPEND ON A PROFESSIONAL AS INSURANCE AGAINST CATASTROPHIC BREACHES.

GUARD A GROWING BUSINESS At last, your business has taken off. So, how do you scale up? The biggest problem for businesses as they grow is that they tend to continue using tools they have instead of reassessing their needs. This is especially true with spending the money to upgrade computers, because business owners don't want to feel like they're getting ripped off: "Why do I need a new firewall? The old one hasn't burned up yet!"

Cyberincident responders see this all the time, even in publicly traded companies—especially ones that have grown quickly. Failures usually fall into two categories. The first one is just that: a failure to properly scope technology requirements and scale technology purchases to match. The second is more insidious: its fast growth, during which executives make decisions to build now and scramble to secure later.

This is the most tempting thing in the world. I can tell you from the painful personal experience of having to break the news to senior executives at Fortune 500 companies that, because of decisions like that ten years previously, the cost to implement a fix is approximately 100 times what it would have been to do it right in the first place. In the security industry, we call this "technical debt," and it's like using a high-interest credit card. You can go ahead and do it, but the day absolutely will come—we guarantee it—when the bank wants its money, and you find out about the wonders of compounding interest. Here's how to avoid that pain.

Get Upgraded Find trustworthy, well-referenced security companies near you and ask them to help you review your needs and make recommendations. These companies are generally easy to check out, and better firms have principals who regularly speak at security conferences, consistently publish articles and write books, and participate in the business community. Find two, and if they generally agree, then go with the one you like most.

Get Tough You'll be looking at a beefed-up version of the secure home office we described. Seek out some kind of centralized authentication system, regular incremental backups and frequent snapshots of your environment, and encryption in every place it can fit. You'll need to hire a good information technology person to manage these systems, or employ a company to manage your infrastructure as a service, an increasingly popular option. You should also consider keeping your critical systems such as servers and firewalls under some form of maintenance contract or support by the vendor. Vulnerabilities in hardware, firmware, and software are constantly disclosed, and having maintenance will keep you up to date without having to either buy new equipment or learn from technical debt bankruptcy.

Get Backup This should go without saying, but back up all your business data . . . and then create a second backup, preferably off-site in a cloud storage server, for example. And then consider a third—just in case. This may sound a little paranoid, but if something goes drastically wrong and you need to restore data, you'll be glad you did.

Get Outside Help Consider hiring a third party to monitor your firewalls and other security gear for signs of trouble. You should have your internal tech person run vulnerability scans regularly so that you keep complete lists of what you actually have and what connects to your network (you won't believe how difficult this is for many companies). Have that double-checked by an outside firm, either regularly as a service or at least once a year.

Get a Checkup Every eighteen months or so, perform a security architecture review. Take this opportunity to reexamine the single most vulnerable part of most business networks: your assumptions. Although taking this step might mean having to pay a bit more up front, it'll be well worth it for the peace of mind it'll bring. As someone who sends his kid to a private boarding school, I can tell you that the alternative is dramatically more expensive in the long run.

KEY CONCEPT

BRICKS AND MORTAR

Any brick-and-mortar shop that has developed a great online presence gets a great benefit from the fact that the cost of maintaining this infrastructure is much cheaper than it used to be: Now, you park the entirety of your business's electronic infrastructure in the cloud instead of maintaining it on-site. But "cloud" does not mean "secure." Cloud infrastructure still has many of the issues of traditional infrastructure, and if you're selling goods online, you have issues of payment card industry compliance to deal with as well. Fortunately, most of this can be outsourced, reducing costs even further. However, it pays to have third-party firms provide you with vulnerability analyses, architecture reviews, and penetration tests—especially against your primary business applications—regularly.

SECURITY BASIC

BACK UP PROPERLY
If utilizing a Windows server, you can turn on shadow copies, which allows you to revert file changes made to the system. This can be done by starting the volume shadow copy service and changing the startup type to automatically via the services in the administrator control panel in the control panel. You can then go to File Explorer, right-click on a drive, go to the shadow copies tab, and enable the option on the drive or on other drives on the system. Shadow copies aren't backups but a quick way to revert files or folders, such as when a user accidently deletes a file or if a few files become encrypted by a crypto malware. You'll need professional help in setting this up, but on the day ransomware encrypts all your files, or all your machines get stolen, it will be worth every penny you spent and then some.

ONLINE BUSINESS BANKING Business banking is where most companies get into trouble. The problem is that banks are not actually responsible for wire transfers and automated clearinghouse transfers made from your business account without your knowledge provided that those transfers were made using your credentials. Business accounts are not protected in the same way that personal ones are. Most banks will still try and help you claw back stolen money, but in some cases where the victim of fraudulent transfers sued the bank, the bank turned around and counter-sued that customer . . . and won.

Keep It Simple Unless you employ more than, say, 250 people, we recommend not using online business banking without an actual two-factor authentication login and a voice verification from the bank. Weirdly, the only banks that seem to offer this without any hassle are not the big guys but the boutique banks.

Get Personal We have found that these smaller banks—the ones that provide personal bankers who know you and your voice, and who ask about your family—are usually the banks with the best possible security you can get. The argument about availability of bank branches is absolutely valid—but with the security upside of the most common vector of attack (wire and ACH fraud) handled, the inconvenience may be worth it. Oh, and we have found that the costs are just about the same between the big banks and the boutiques.

No matter what kind of online banking you prefer, we recommend using a dedicated computer for it. The less that computer interacts with the public internet, the less of a chance there is of your credentials being hijacked.

A SECURE WEBSITE A business without a website is simply not taken seriously. Where people get into trouble is trying to build an e-commerce website on the cheap. That is a guaranteed disaster—note, I didn't say almost a guarantee. It's rock solid. If you want to sell things on your website, you need to understand that one of the internet's most vulnerable things is the commercial web application.

The good news is that if you're just looking for a basic web presence—a site consisting of a home page, contacts, information about your services or products, and that sort of thing—there are a lot of very cheap options out there that are in fact quite beautiful and professional looking. Right now, I'm partial to Squarespace. They have designs you can personalize, and you pay a monthly charge for them to host it. They even make it very easy to buy your domain name—all these things that vexed your predecessors in the 1990s and aughts have been reduced to wizard-based menus.

Beyond any design aesthetics and good customer service you've built in, there are also some important guidelines to creating and maintaining a properly secure business website.

Stay Secure First, make sure your site itself, when built, is a secured one. This means your site's address will have an https prefix instead of just http, along with a small padlock icon. This adds a layer of encryption and makes it harder for hackers to break in. Further layers of security, such as a web application firewall (WAF), will add to your protection. A "secure and verified" badge added to your site, when clicked on, will also provide full verification to visitors, including the date of the last security scan.

Keep It Up to Date Whether you build your site yourself or trust someone else to do it, keep your software updated. New exploits are found on a weekly basis, and you don't want to become the latest victim of something like the 2017 WannaCry attack in which computers that hadn't installed a basic security update were hijacked to attack hospitals, phone companies, and others in 150 nations.

Run a Tight Ship Change passwords often, and keep them strong. Hide and rename admin directories in your business website to thwart any hackers, as they invariably will go after files and folders with names such as "admin" and "login."

Be Transparent Display your business's privacy policies on your website, explaining what data is collected, how it is secured, and what is done in the event of a breach; update your policy as needed.

GOOD TO KNOW

A STRONG DEFENSE
IT security is best done in layers; the more there are, the harder it is to have unauthorized access. No matter the OS, no single silver bullet will keep you secure. So, what to do? Turn on the firewall built into the OS. Inaccessible application port connections reduce security risk. Update software regularly, not just automatic updates, and keep antivirus software to protect your machine and data, including against malware. Disable remote access if unneeded. Use 2FA and VPNs through a company firewall with support agreements (to add content filtering, remote access, constant updates, and malware protection). Keep Wi-Fi separate and protected, and employ intrusion monitoring along with virtual LANs. Control with whom files are shared, consider security awareness training, and, last, keep all hardware in a secure room with restricted access.

GOOD TO KNOW

REPUTATION REPAIR
Let's say people are leaving bad reviews of your business on Yelp or Google. Instead of hiring services to try and "fix" your reputation, go online and answer questions and concerns. If a negative review on Yelp is followed by your side of the story and an offer to make things right, people tend to cut you some slack.

Real, useful content that shows your business in a positive light is often weighted more than complaints and slander by search engines. That said, if you're an executive who said something untoward on Twitter, for example, and the story is picked up by the press, you're in for a few years of reputation building. In this case, a reputation repair service might take some of the weight off of you. But there is no way to erase stuff from the internet: Work on new, relevant, accessible content that search engines will value more than the bad stuff.

LOSING IT BIG TIME

It's hard to do a scientific ranking of corporate heists, partly because the information is rarely made public, and partly because it's hard to attribute dollar values. That said, here are some major breaches.

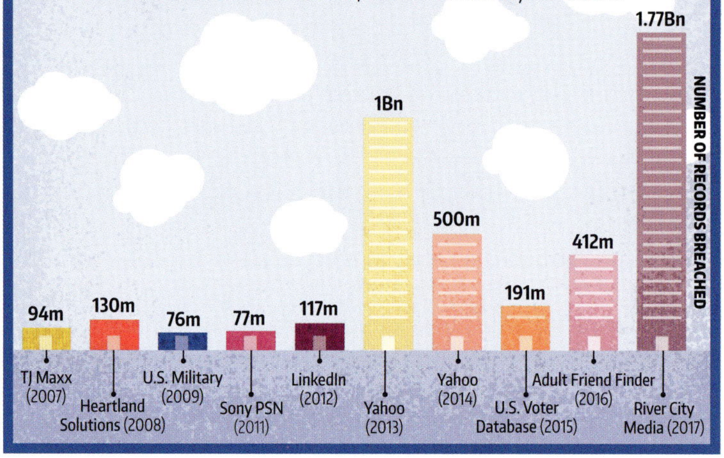

ORGANIZED RETAIL CRIME When people watch the news and see a breaking story announcing that, say, fifty million peoples' credit card data was stolen from Target or Home Depot, they sometimes wonder, "Just what the hell can you do with fifty million stolen credit card numbers?" The answer is simple: You can sell them to other criminals—in blocks of 1,000 card numbers at a time.

Criminal Coding Criminals can monetize stolen cards in any number of ways, but one popular method involves gangs of crooks who buy a bunch of stolen credit cards and a magnetic card encoder (similar to the kind used to make hotel room keys). They pay people to obtain cards of all kinds with magnetic stripes: used gift cards, used hotel room keys, stolen credit cards—anything with a stripe. Then the perps re-encode them with the information from the stolen cards.

A Larcenous Road Trip Once the cards are coded the gang rents a moving truck, assembles a small team of accomplices, and drives along an interstate highway until they come to a shopping mall. After giving each of the team a little stack of the re-encoded cards, the leader sends them on their merry way into the mall, with instructions to use those cards to buy things under a certain amount—say, $500 USD—and bring them back to the truck. If a given card doesn't work, they simply throw it away and swipe another one, working their way through the mall and through the stack of cards at the same time.

When they're done at one mall, they drive to another. Soon, they have a truck full of swag. And at some point, the swag gets sold on eBay or other online outlets.

There's big money to be made, and that's one of the reasons banks and credit-card companies rolled out chip + PIN cards, designed to combat exactly this kind of point-of-sale scam. This development means that criminals will have to find some new way to rip of card-holders and businesses. I have faith in their ingenuity.

THE TAKEAWAY

Head spinning with all the ways someone might try to rip off or otherwise undermine your small (or not so small) business?. Check these basics.

BASIC SECURITY

- Encrypt, back up, and use strong passwords for data. Hire professionals to help set up systems.
- Delete as much information as you can every week; you can't lose data you don't have.
- Use a cloud-based service to back up your minimal set of business data.
- Teach your employees best security practices and policies.
- Train any employee authorized to transfer money about inviolate procedures for wire transfers.

ADVANCED MEASURES

- Employ two-factor authentication and do vulnerability and penetration tests regularly.
- Take snapshots of all computers at least daily, if not more often, and store them encrypted in the cloud.
- Have a plan in place in case any of your business-related devices are compromised, lost, or destroyed.
- Run quarterly tabletop exercises to practice the plan and find problems with it.

TINFOIL-HAT BRIGADE

- Keep single-sign-on, forced-VPN, all-virtual desktops.
- Run phishing awareness and other security programs as training for your staff.
- Keep an incident-response company on retainer.

*

HALF OF ALL SMALL BUSINESSES HAVE A SECURITY BREACH EACH YEAR. PROTECT DATA WITH SIMPLE ENCRYPTION AND GOOD PASSWORDS. A BREACH RUINS CUSTOMER TRUST. SPEND BEFORE, NOT AFTER, THE BREACH.

CHAPTER 2

THE FUTURE OF MONEY

THESE DAYS THE PHRASE "NEW MONEY" HAS COME TO MEAN A PORTFOLIO OF VIRTUAL CURRENCIES. IN A WORLD WHERE MONEY IS JUST A SERIES OF ONES AND ZEROES, HOW DO YOU KEEP YOUR ELECTRONIC PENNIES SAFE?

Throughout history humankind has relied on some form of currency, using everything from shells to gold to make purchases. The island of Manhattan was even bought with a bag of beads not so long ago. We use it every day, but we tend not to think much about the concept of money beyond whether we have enough. In fact, the idea that we've agreed that these pieces of paper and metal represent real value that can be traded for pizzas and underpants is quite remarkable. Over the centuries, things have changed at a blinding pace in the world of money, and it won't slow down anytime soon.

In the 1960s and '70s, modern credit cards were introduced, bringing with them a whole host of new and exciting ways for criminals to steal your money. Some banks were so trusting of their customers that they didn't even do credit checks . . . they just mailed out these shiny new cards and assumed that the recipients would be sensible. That went about as well as you might imagine. And that was before anyone had the technology to skim those digits, recode them onto a hotel card key, and go to town. Now, digital banking services like PayPal and ApplePay, and the brave new world of digital currencies like bitcoin (BTC), mean there are even more ways to steal your scratch.

CASH FREE I recently went to Australia on a two-week business trip. As an experiment, I wanted to see if I could go the entire trip without using any Australian currency. To my surprise, I discovered that I could! I used my credit card for the majority of my transactions. (To Australia's credit, it has one of the most innovative payment industries in the world; the country has adopted new payment technology that makes a purchase as easy as waving your credit card over a terminal.) I used various apps on my mobile phone to pay for my transportation. Each of these apps had previously saved my payment details, so they automatically billed me in my native currency. At one point, I actually needed cash for a purchase, but I just happened to have some U.S. dollars in my wallet, and the small-business merchant agreed to accept them.
—Heather Vescent

FUN FACT

LIVING ON BITCOINS In 2013, reporter Kashmir Hill wondered whether she could live for a week paying for things only in bitcoin. She had trouble finding vendors who would accept Bitcoin for services and many hadn't heard of the new currency. When she tried the experiment the following year, after several start-ups had made it easier for merchants to accept bitcoin, she was able to use a ride-sharing service and pay for a seventeen-course dinner. So yes, while you can purchase cupcakes, lunch, coffee, and even a mani-pedi on Wilshire Boulevard in Los Angeles with bitcoin, it's not the norm by any means. It's still mostly a novelty for many, although there was plenty of buzz about bitcoin a few years ago, when it was at the peak of the hype cycle. And today there are those who believe that digital currency can still change the world.

A CURRENCY REVOLUTION The idea of cryptocurrencies kicked off in 1998, with an essay written by computer engineer and cypherpunk Wei Dai that envisioned a form of money created and controlled by cryptography instead of a central government. In 2008, a pseudonymous developer operating under the name Satoshi Nakamoto released an open-source white paper describing a peer-to-peer method for creating a cryptocurrency called bitcoin. In the beginning, the only attention it received was from a small group of crypto enthusiasts. Now, bitcoin has kicked off a currency revolution and re-envisioned money for the information age.

How Is Bitcoin Made? Unlike physical money, no one person or government owns the technology or concept behind bitcoin. New bitcoins are generated by people on the internet who competitively work to record and verify previous bitcoin transactions—starting from the very first transaction in 2009—in a process called mining. Think of it as using your computer's processing power to solve a complex puzzle. Whoever solves a step (or block) in the mining process is rewarded with a new amount of bitcoin.

Is Bitcoin Actually Money? The U.S. government sees bitcoin as a commodity rather than a currency, but many use it for transactions as if it were money. Its value fluctuates, generally trending up as the number of new coins decreases, and acts like a stock at times, rising and falling based on perceived value. In 2009, the first bitcoin was valued at $0.07 USD, but it soared as high as $1,250 in 2017.

Will Bitcoin Replace Other Currency? Early on, many speculated that bitcoin could replace nation-state-backed money such as the U.S. dollar. Once it was released into the wild internet, it took on a life of its own and attracted a different set of users, forcing governments to react (with the U.S. government classifying it as a commodity, for example). Nevertheless, it started a revolution—showing a viable new way of creating currency for the digital age.

Is Bitcoin Anonymous? One of the "features" of bitcoin is the ability to complete anonymous transactions. But this isn't totally accurate. Financial institutions require compliance with KYC ("know your customer") regulation, so if you buy bitcoins from an exchange where you have a connected financial institution, your wallet can be traced to your identity. However, there are ways to set up anonymous wallets. In either case, the transactions are recorded on the blockchain.

NOTABLE CRYPTOCURRENCIES

There are hundreds of cryptocurrencies out there. Most are copycats or have been developed to expand initial bitcoin functionality. Here are a few examples.

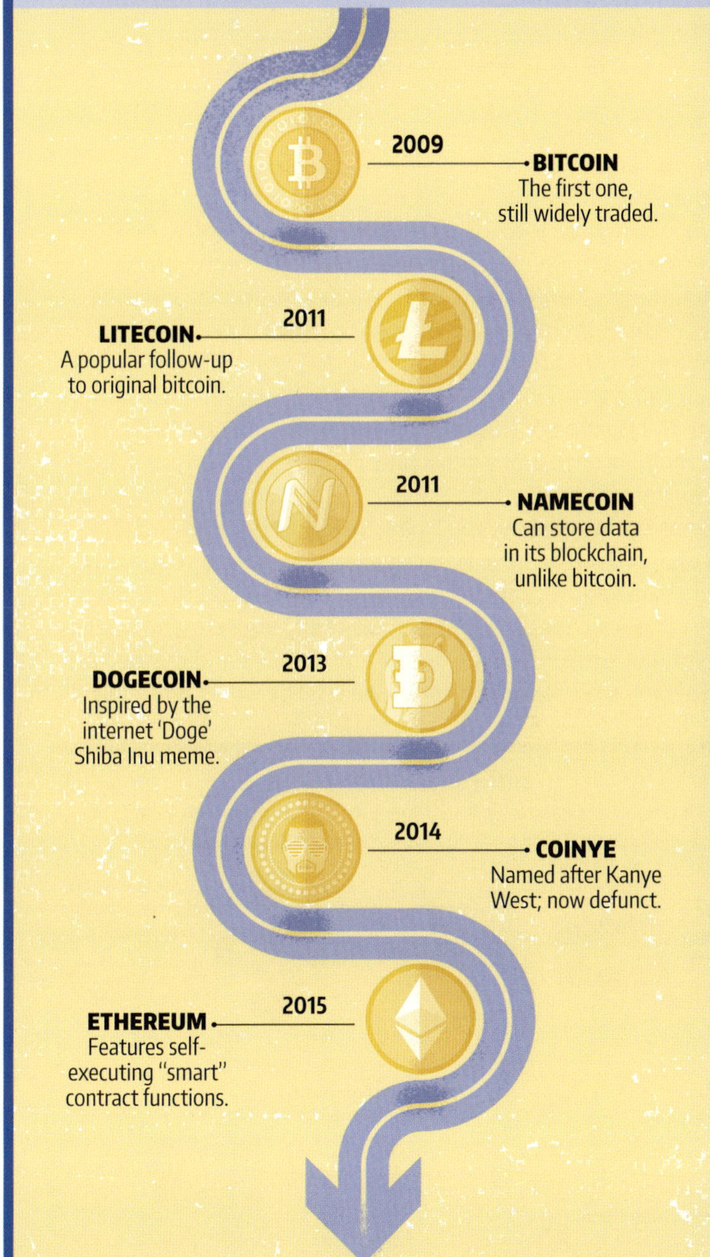

TRUE STORY

ELECTRONIC HEISTS

New currencies, like all new technology, are experiments and not secure or fully tested. When you put your skin in this game, you could lose it. In 2013, Bloomberg TV hosted a bitcoin special, wherein host Matt Miller gave anchors Adam Johnson and Trish Regan a code that would give them $20 each in BTC. A fast-thinking viewer used the code on the TV screen, effectively snatching it from Johnson's hands when he showed it to the studio camera.

Larger losses have also happened. Mt. Gox, based in Tokyo, was one of the first bitcoin exchanges. At one point, it handled 70 percent of the world's bitcoin trades. In 2013, it took up to months for customers to withdraw funds, halting operations several times before closing in February 2014. Through bankruptcy filings, it was discovered the company stole as many as 650,000 bitcoins from customers.

KEY CONCEPT

THE BLOCKCHAIN All bitcoin transactions that take place are recorded on the blockchain—a database that acts as a public ledger and helps to reinforce the cryptography behind the currency. Transactions are each recorded with a time stamp, the amount of transaction, the wallet address that sent the bitcoins, and the address that received it.

With cash transactions, no one knows the details of your actions. With bitcoin, a certain number of transactions are formalized into a "block." When each new block is recorded on the previous block, the transaction data is set in stone and can't be changed. The blockchain is the ultimate tracking system—it's decentralized, no one can manipulate it, and any information added to a blockchain is also permanently recorded. Because the blockchain records are set in stone, it reduces the bitcoin's full anonymity.

MONETARY MYSTERIES AND ELECTRONIC INTRIGUE As cryptocurrencies continue to develop, so too do the questions behind them. For example, no one has yet discovered the true identity of Satoshi Nakamoto—possibly a pseudonym for a single person or a collective group who worked on the idea of bitcoin together. Whether Nakamoto is an individual or a group, the introduction of bitcoin has changed the way we look at money and its relation to the internet forever.

Investing in Cryptocurrencies Those who are curious about bitcoin and other cryptocurrencies can acquire them in multiple ways. The original method is to join in the mining effort, which means using your own computer and a set of specialized software (and sometimes extra hardware) to work on the blockchain, and thus unlock the next set of bitcoins by solving it. Don't be surprised if it takes a while, though: Mining on your own is akin to playing the lottery, while mining in a group (or pool) means getting a return equal to the fraction of the pool's computing power that you've put in. Multiple exchanges are online, and you can also purchase cryptocurrencies from other people.

No matter the method, you'll have to use an address—a public string of numbers—to send or receive bitcoins, similar to the way that an email address handles messages. A wallet is actually just a private string of code that corresponds to the address, and stores the cryptocurrency info, keeping the bitcoins safe and reached only to the person who has access to the wallet. The wallet is not usually

DOING THE LAUNDRY

It is relatively easy to obscure the source of cryptocurrencies used in illegal or otherwise shady transactions. Here's how it's done.

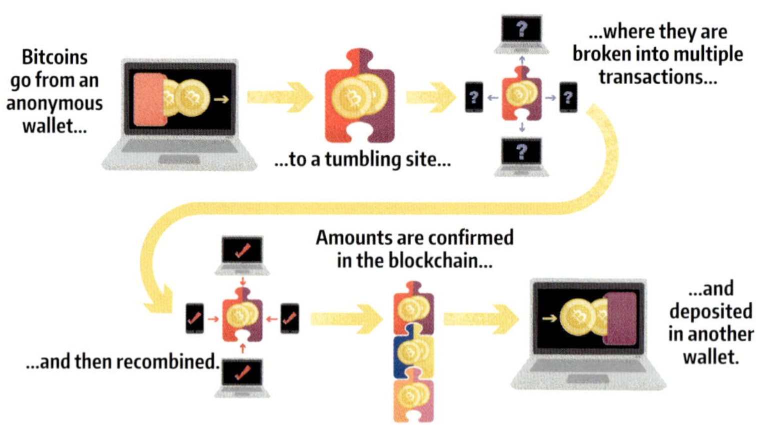

physical—although some people do indeed keep access to these digital wallets on a physical object, such as a USB stick, to reduce the risk of losing cryptocurrency in a hack.

Convenience or Anonymity? If you buy bitcoins from an online exchange, they will give you your own address and wallet. Once you have connected your bank account and once it's been confirmed as yours, you can buy bitcoins from the exchange, storing them there on their in-house wallet, or you can export them to an outside address. As an investment, bitcoin and all cryptocurrencies are high-risk. Bitcoins have been stolen, and legitimate exchanges have gone bankrupt and customers have lost their bitcoins. In order to have a totally anonymous bitcoin wallet, you will have to resort to buying the bitcoins in person—yes, this means that you'll have to physically hand someone cash. They will then send bitcoins to your anonymous wallet. Since cash transactions are not tracked, you can have them transferred to a wallet that has no identity associated with it. (The electronic transaction will be recorded in the blockchain, regardless.)

Bitcoin and Black Markets Up to this point we have discussed the legitimate uses for bitcoin. But plenty of people out there also utilize bitcoin for illicit transactions, money laundering, or moving money around in ways that can't be easily tracked. There are innumerable black markets, and the most popular and active ones are always changing as old ones are shut down and new ones pop up. The first and most notorious online black market was called Silk Road, and it was started by the Dread Pirate Roberts in 2011. Functioning much like eBay, Silk Road offered illegal and prescription drugs, hacked data, fake IDs, and more. Silk Road was shut down by the FBI in late 2013, and the Dread Pirate was unmasked as Ross William Ulbricht, who is now serving a lifetime prison sentence (see pages 64–65 for more on his strange tale).

The Future of Cryptocurrency In all likelihood, bitcoin and other cryptocurrencies will stick around for some time to come. The way has been paved for modern digital currency experiments, putting pressure on the traditional financial transaction methods to reduce bank and transfer fees, while increasing transfer speeds. Although we will see more characteristics of this technology as part of our existing currencies in the future, it won't entirely replace the U.S. dollar for groceries and gas anytime soon. Cryptocurrency values fluctuate too frequently, governments see them as commodities at best, and the technology will continue to be targeted for hacks.

T/F

YOU CAN LAUNDER MONEY WITH BITCOIN

TRUE When you use cash to buy bitcoins from someone in person, there is no trail. Bitcoin wallets are not required to have identifiable information. An anonymous email address can be used to start a wallet, which can then hold bitcoins. If you end up with a large sum of bitcoins and want to cash out, you can find someone to exchange them. The trick is to keep identity data away from these bitcoin wallets. Cash transactions aren't recorded, so it makes using bitcoins to launder money appealing. There are also "tumblers," programs or sites that mingle fractions of BTC in multiple transactions. After a time, the bitcoins come out clean—well, at least in theory.

FUN FACT

MOBILE MINUTES AS MONEY Currency is essentially a physical representation of value. Historically, gold and other precious metals and minerals have been used as a medium of exchange based on their rarity and perceived actual value. It makes sense that anything of mutual value between parties can be used as money. In several parts of Africa, technology has taken the place of bills and coins: Savvy entrepreneurs have been using mobile airtime as a currency, such as the M-Pesa system in Kenya, which allows the exchange of money and airtime. Prepaid mobile phone cards are used instead of bills, and mobile phone owners rent out phones or barter minutes for goods and services. Given their near-universal utility, mobile minutes are considered more sound than many regional currencies subject to a government's stability or economic fluctuations.

TECHNOLOGY AND MONEY As our technology evolves, so will our finances. From IOUs to ledgers to consistent coins and bank notes, it makes perfect sense that as our technology improves, we would apply it to money.

Smartphones and Finances Anyone with a smartphone basically carries a tiny computer in their pocket and can connect to the global financial network. Whether you are making a bank transfer, sending a PayPal payment, making a trade, buying a tomato at a farmers' market, calling for a ride share, or paying with bitcoin through a QR code, today's mobile phones are more sophisticated than the bank tellers of twenty years ago.

Credit Cards One of the money dreams of the future is the creation of a single global unified currency. We already have that today in a way, thanks to credit cards that are accepted almost everywhere and have excellent fraud protection. But even with the best security system, sophisticated social hackers can successfully impersonate you despite the strictest precautions. Credit cards are never going away and are a de facto universal currency.

Blockchain Expansion While they may sometimes vary in perceived value between curiosity and commodity, cryptocurrencies aren't going anywhere anytime soon—and neither is the blockchain. In fact, the concept of the blockchain can be applied to other parts of the world's economy, and not just for tracking of cryptocurrencies and the transactions they are used in. As the transactions on a blockchain are set in stone once recorded, the technology could be used to create cheap, tamper-proof public registries of who owns various land or property, notarize documents without the need for a notary on-site, and even ensure the security and value of stock market and other high-value trading systems and financial transactions.

Smart Contracts Ethereum, one of the more notable cryptocurrencies, was created by Vitalik Buterin, who wanted to build applications on top of the (bitcoin) blockchain. Since he could not add this extension to bitcoin, he launched Ethereum. The big innovation with this cryptocurrency is its ability to write contracts—bits of code execute on their own when certain conditions are met. On Ethereum, developers can write their own smart contracts. In the future, we can imagine a world where a piece of software initiates a financial transaction once certain conditions are met. Smart contracts could be used for human transactions, but more likely they will be used for computer-to-computer payment transactions.

Financial Intelligences It's not far-fetched to imagine software making transactions on your behalf. Automated bill paying already exists, which lets you set your bank account to make payments on your behalf. As we develop better intelligence, personal financial intelligence may someday go further.

In the future, we can expect our technology to take care of the financial transactions entirely. This is something that is already happening with services like Airbnb, Lyft, and Uber, which have the payment aspect built into the software app experience, removing it completely from the real-world experience. Amazon has done something similar with its innovative physical stores, where you can walk out with the items you want and are automagically charged for the items you selected instead of having to check out.

In the end, the future of money must include more security and convenience while being easy to use. As technology continues to innovate, we will also have to keep up with bugs, flaws, and loopholes, fixing them as they arise.

KEY CONCEPT

KNOW YOUR CUSTOMER Any financial institution out there has to have a degree of security, stability, and trustworthiness in order to operate, and that includes having stable customers. Traditional banking regulations require banks to know their customers (called "KYC" in bankspeak). To comply with these financing regulations, banks have to confirm the identities of all their account holders. When you open some bitcoin wallets, especially any that are connected to traditional bank accounts, you may have to prove your identity. It's not recommended to do illicit transactions or make black-market purchases with these accounts—unless you want to increase the chance of being busted. However, there are other ways to acquire bitcoin that do keep the purchases anonymous and can also facilitate money laundering.

GOOD TO KNOW

SMART MONEY, SMART THIEVES

You might think that increasing surveillance and face-recognition software would help catch the guy who stole your wallet, especially with all the cameras out there. But the problem is accessing the data before it's deleted and then taking action on it.

In the case of Quentin Hardy, whose wallet was stolen in San Francisco, the thief used his stolen credit card for Uber. The card was connected to an existing account, and since Uber keeps data on all its rides, it had info about the thief—including GPS data that might show where the thief lived. The problem with this is getting the data, which often can only be legally released to the enforcement, and the infraction has to be big enough to warrant an investigation. Often, it is not. And even so, by the time the police get around to seeing the video footage, it may have already been deleted.

DIGITAL SAFEKEEPING In the future, we won't get to simply stash our cash in a safe or under a mattress. New forms of finance mean new protocols for keeping your money safe.

Keeping Online Integrity While many governments offer individual reimbursements from fraud, business accounts are not always guaranteed the same security, and online banking and fraud protection are not typically in the hands of the user. Look for financial institutions that have good security—sometimes it's hard to find out which ones have been hacked, because no one wants to disclose that information. Use robust passwords in online banking, change them often, and don't reuse old passwords. Limit who you share banking authentication credentials with to reduce the chance of unauthorized transfers or transactions.

Stay Secure with a Selfie Banks are motivated to use secure systems. Passwords can be difficult to enter on a mobile device, so banks have other secure authentication systems options: your fingerprint, a PIN, or facial (or even voice) recognition. The secure selfie is even hacker proof—you must blink or make a facial gesture that you can't duplicate with a photograph.

Be Safer with Biometrics Biometric verification has been thought of as the great fail-safe. The idea is that it's near impossible to replicate someone's fingerprint or iris or retina, although hackers (and Hollywood) have shown ways to duplicate a fingerprint. Unlike a password reset, it's not that easy to get a new fingertip or eye. There are, however, security combinations that use hashed biometric data for three-factor (adding a biometric to the password and token) or even four-factor identity verification involving a second biometric. The more factors that are required for a transaction, the harder it is for a thief to steal or replicate them.

Practice Credit Control Use multiple credit accounts. The first is for automatic monthly payments; the second (with a low limit) for spontaneous online purchases and the like (this number can be virtual, or even single use, so you have to get new ones each time you want to use the account); and a third for physical shopping, with a slightly higher credit limit. Monitor your credit score. You'll know if there is a change in your score and be empowered to fix it. Check your bank accounts on a regular basis via a dashboard or phone app, and set up notification for certain transactions and amounts. Tell your bank or credit company when you are traveling so it will allow your purchases. Know your bank's customer service numbers and how to stop payments or authorize a charge on your mobile app.

BIOMETRIC AUTHENTICATION METHODS

You can use more than just fingerprints for confirming someone's identity—and more means are developing all the time.

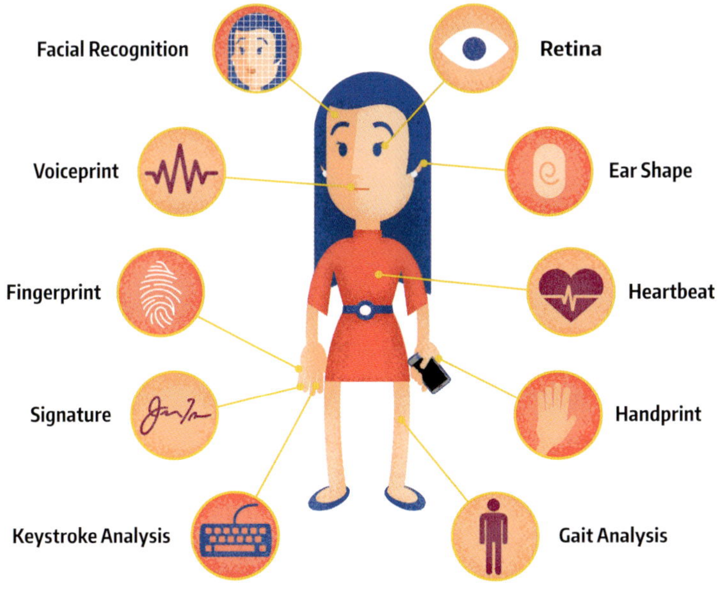

T/F

CHIP AND PIN CARDS CAN'T BE HACKED.

FALSE Chip and PIN credit cards were first released in the United States in 2015 to decrease fraud and identity theft. But it turns out that they are not as secure as we might think. In Europe, to use a chip and PIN card, the PIN is entered at the point of sale. This would make impersonation very difficult—or would it? In 2015 in Europe, a creative team of criminals devised a man-in-the-middle attack by soldering a different chip onto the card, which was then able to accept any PIN entered. To manage such sophisticated card hacking required a certain level of know-how, skill, and artistry—but it was one that ultimately resulted in the thieves getting $680,000 USD worth of free goods.

FUN FACTS

BIG LOSERS Big money plus gambling can mean big losses. You can try to blame it on the free drinks—which is what Mark Johnston tried to do when he lost $500,000 USD one weekend in Las Vegas, saying he was black-out drunk—to avoid paying gambling losses. Then there's the story of the CEO of the Oriental Trading Company, Terrance Watanabe, who lost $127 million USD at Harrah's in 2007 and accused the casino of giving him pain medication and keeping his glass full. (He was also known to play three hands of blackjack at the same time.) Meanwhile, a software bug on a Eurobet website caused Bruno Venturi to make £650,000 from £17—but the company refused to pay, citing the software bug. And Harry Kakavas from Australia lost $1.5 billion AUD in just over a year and attempted to sue, claiming casinos took advantage of his status as a compulsive gambler. Play responsibly!

GAMBLING AND THE INTERNET We would be remiss in discussing the internet and money if we didn't also include a throw of the electronic dice. It used to be that if you wanted to try to get rich quick (or more likely just waste your money), you had to go hit the slots and tables in places like Las Vegas or Atlantic City or Reno—or maybe find a smoky back room for an underground poker game. These days, you only have to go as far as your home computer. That dicey place where the internet and your finances intersect is in online gambling, and while you won't have to worry about ending the night smelling of cigar smoke out of your hair or avoid having a cocktail spilled on your suit, internet poker or roulette or slots carry plenty of their own risks and concerns.

Living with the Law Depending on where you are in the world, local laws restrict gambling online as well as in person, especially in the United States. the Federal Wire Act of 1961 has been construed by courts to mean that it covers all forms of gambling. The FBI may not break down your door if you bet a dollar on that online poker forum, but the legal risks are still present, as well as dealing with the tax issues should you win big.

Supporting Your Local Mob There are plenty of historical ties among gambling, casinos, and organized crime, and internet gambling is no exception. Plenty of gambling sites are relatively legitimate, but it's just as likely that a given online casino could also be a place where money is being laundered and other shady dealings are being supported behind the scenes.

Going for Broke The biggest risk associated with gambling is losing all your money or developing an addiction, or both. Humans tend to respond strongly to game-of-chance situations, due to a psychological effect called intermittent reward: If you don't know when to expect the payout from a gamble, there's a chance you'll keep trying over and over. And if you can go for that potential reward without having to leave your house and visit a casino, you could easily empty your savings account while still in your pajamas.

Making Your Loss Their Profit Whether the risk is tied to organized crime or no, internet gambling requires spending money, either by transferring funds from a bank account or providing a credit card number or some other means of sharing your financial information. If a gambling site you're visiting gets hacked and you have any information saved there (or any money left in an account on-site), then you run the risk of getting your finances stolen.

THE TAKEAWAY

Putting your money where your modem is opens you up to all kinds of new and exciting financial risks. Here are some methods of staying safer while spending online.

BASIC SECURITY	• Monitor your accounts. • Set up alerts for your accounts and for purchases over a certain amount. • Use a strong password, and don't use the same password for multiple accounts. • Use a stronger password for your financial accounts than anywhere else.
ADVANCED MEASURES	• Use multifactor authentication. • Use credit cards that offer fraud protection and identity protection. • Monitor your credit score.
TINFOIL-HAT BRIGADE	• Use financial services that offer biometrics, or three- (or four-) factor authentication. • "Launder" your cryptocurrency by using services that obscure the source. • Use cryptocurrency like a one-time pad: buy the coin, launder it, make your purchase, and erase all records.

STATE AND LOCAL LAWS CAN AND DO OUTLAW VARIOUS FORMS OF ONLINE GAMBLING. CHECK YOUR LOCAL LAWS, BECAUSE SOME PROHIBIT ANY TRANSACTION INVOLVING GAMBLING SITES.

DEGREES OF DECEPTION

EACH YEAR, PHONY SCHOOLS RAKE IN BILLIONS OF DOLLARS FROM UNSUSPECTING OR EVEN CRIMINAL STUDENTS WHO MIGHT THEN END UP IN CHARGE OF NUCLEAR REACTORS, NATIONAL SECURITY, OR YOUR EMERGENCY HEART SURGERY.

The very first universities that granted academic degrees to their students were established in Europe in the eleventh century. It should come as no great surprise that, not too long thereafter, the first counterfeit degrees began appearing as well. In America, fake schools were awarding degrees long before the Revolutionary War. But why should we fret if a Renaissance count or a gentleman farmer bought the right to call himself "Doctor" without doing any work? Historians are probably the only ones who care about those cases, but everyone should be concerned when, as happened recently, a highly placed (and unqualified) Homeland Security official and a top nuclear engineer turned out to have purchased their degrees. Fake college degrees are held by tens of thousands of deceptive doctors, lawyers, therapists, teachers, and others whom we count on to be well trained. And that doesn't include the thousands more noncriminal but naive degree holders who simply fell for a fast-talking salesperson who convinced them to lay down heaps of money for nothing more than a worthless piece of paper—one that may, in fact, be a lot worse than worthless. A fake degree can be a career-ender if it should be exposed—and that's to say nothing of the risk to others before the truth comes out.

FOREIGN EXCHANGE How do any of these degree mills actually receive legitimacy or accreditation? In one example, in 2003, the government of Liberia—at the time considered corrupt, unstable, and nearly bankrupt—wrote to a number of questionable schools offering them the full accreditation of the Liberian Ministry of Education for the low, low price of $1,000 USD (later raised to $10,000, and then increased once more to $50,000 down and $20,000 a year). In short order, more than a dozen non-wonderful schools, most of them located within the borders of the United States, were proudly advertising their certificates of accreditation—signed by a legit minister of education from a nation that's unquestionably a member of the United Nations. That situation was eventually resolved legally through UNESCO, but there's nothing to stop it from happening again elsewhere.

FUN FACTS

3,300 Estimated number of fake or substandard universities worldwide

50,000 Number of fake PhDs bought each year in the United States (more than the 45,000 earned legitimately)

5,000 Number of fake medical doctors identified by a Congressional sub-committee

100,000 Estimated number of United States federal employees with fake degrees

$300,000,000 USD Value of worldwide sales of false degrees each year

$1 USD Lowest cost of a fake degree (excepting those thrown in as a bonus for larger orders)

0 Hours of study required for the average fake degree (if the check clears)

3 Number of James Bond movies students needed to watch to earn a degree from the late Eastern Caribbean University

BUYING FROM DIPLOMA MILLS People purchase degrees for any number of reasons, but the following are the most common.

Employment Opportunities Many jobs will require that people in certain positions have a specific degree (or, sometimes, any degree), which can lead job hunters to fake it. Others believe that the esteem of an advanced degree will give them an advantage in the market.

Professional Prestige While a marriage counselor doesn't need to have a doctorate, a financial planner an MBA, or a contractor a degree in engineering, being able to advertise those degrees may attract more customers or inspire more confidence from clients.

Professional Validation You've worked hard all your life. Why shouldn't you get the recognition you deserve? This is a valid argument, as the practice of credit for "life experience" illustrates. But all too often, this line of thought is used by fake schools to convince potential students that rewarding their hard work with a phony degree is totally logical—on par with earning a real degree via a legitimate proper education.

DUE DILIGENCE So, what if you suspect that someone you've encountered has faked or fraudulently obtained their college credentials? If it's your old Uncle Morty talking up his suspicious-sounding degree in film studies to win an argument, maybe you can just roll your eyes and let it go. But if the phony degree could have real consequences for the health or safety of others, you should check it out. Looking into the details of a school can also give you reason to steer clear of it if it proves to be an imposter.

GOOD TO KNOW

FALSE WITNESS One of the more frightening subsets of prestige, or being seen as an authority in a particular field, is the matter of expert witnesses in court cases. A lot of damage can be done—but the courts rarely seem to check the legitimacy of those witnesses. Indeed, this author, Dr. John Bear, has provided expert testimony in dozens of cases of academic fraud; to the best of his knowledge, no one has ever checked his credentials. But this negligence has had serious real-world effects.

The Case of the Fake Engineer One particular self-styled automotive engineer testified on the behalf of an auto manufacturer that the brakes on a vehicle involved in a fatal accident "could not have failed." This man was later exposed on the witness stand as having bought his credentials from a notorious degree mill.

Adulterated Architecture 115 people died when a skyscraper collapsed in a 2011 New Zealand earthquake; the building's designer faked his engineering credentials.

Environmental Hazard We learned of an asbestos removal "expert" whose degrees in environmental science came from a worthless source, rendering all of the "improvements" he'd recommended suspect.

Burn Notice A certain burn expert always concluded that the terribly injured burn victims involved in cases where he was asked to testify had caused their own injuries, and that his corporate clients were not responsible. His fake PhD in safety was at last exposed, triggering a review of cases in which his testimony had been crucial.

Liar, Liar One high-profile lie-detector expert who had appeared on *Larry King Live*, *Geraldo*, and other talk shows, and who was also involved with the O.J. Simpson and JonBenét Ramsey cases, held a doctorate from a notorious degree mill.

T/F

MY DOCTOR MIGHT BE A PHONY

TRUE Terrifying as the concept is, thousands of people have purchased fake medical degrees and are using them to prey on unsuspecting patients. one of the most horrific examples is that of Michail Sorodsky, who bought a phony medical degree, set himself up as a "holistic healer," and, in 2011, was convicted of sexually assaulting women who came to him for treatment. Some of them later died of untreated cancer. Many other deaths and injuries at the hands of fake doctors have been documented over the years—and those are just the ones who got caught. After all, you've probably seen all those framed degrees on your doctor's wall. But have you ever fact-checked them?

KEY CONCEPT

NONSTANDARD SCHOOLS Not every nontraditional school out there is a bad one—some are just, well, not traditional. One thing to be aware of is that shady schools may well use the cover of one of these legitimate alternatives to disguise their own lack of a proper curriculum.

New Ideas Educational models change—not long ago the idea of earning a degree online was crazy. Now it's standard. But beware of schools that claim that they are too innovative to be accredited.

Religious Studies Many totally legit religious schools consider secular academic accreditation to be irrelevant to their mission.

Geographic Variations Standards and practices vary by nation, and even by state in the United States. Some schools game this by claiming a location most favorable to their business model.

CHECK OUT A SCHOOL Some fake schools are highly sophisticated in their advertising and employ expert salespeople to convince wary would-be enrollees to take the plunge. It's not uncommon, when a fake school is exposed, for its customers to be chagrined, saying they should have known better but the salesperson was so convincing, the catalog so shiny, the website so nicely done that they got sucked in. Of course, one of the best possible ways to check out a school is to make an in-person visit, but if that were cheap or easy, online learning wouldn't be so popular.

CONSULT THE PROPER AUTHORITY In the United States, every state has a higher-education agency or the equivalent; most countries have either a single national ministry or a similar situation. An agency will rarely comment on the quality of a school, but it will let you know whether it is properly licensed. Some fake schools go as far as setting up a fake accrediting agency that, miraculously, only have one client, or worse, also accredits Harvard and Yale (without their knowledge), so make sure you find the relevant office through the official U.S. Department of Education website at www2.ed.gov/about/contacts/state/index.html or your nation's equivalent agency.

DO A LITTLE DETECTIVE WORK Some fake schools are clever and sophisticated. Some . . . less so. Here are a few simple first steps to take.

Call Them A sketchy-sounding voicemail during business hours, or a sleepy kid at 3 a.m. their time, is not a good sign.

Click Learning who owns the school's website can be a very rich source of information, especially if it conflicts with what is said by the school itself. www.whois.net is the place to do this.

Zoom In Check the school's address on Google Maps or Google Earth. If you find a mailbox rental store, a WeWork space, or (as we saw recently) a Holiday Inn, it's probably not a top-notch university.

ASK SOME QUESTIONS If you've done the basic checking noted above and you're still not really sure how legit a school is, asking the following questions can help clear things up.

How Many Students Are Enrolled? Quite a few schools seem reluctant to reveal these numbers. Sometimes it's because they're embarrassed about how large they are, as in, for example, the case of one less-than-wonderful school that at one time had more than 3,000 students and a faculty of five. Sometimes the school may be embarrassed about how small it is, as in the case of one highly advertised school that had impressive literature, very high tuition . . . and fewer than 50 students.

How Many Degrees Do You Award Each Year? As with number of students, the answer might be strangely high (as in, as long as

FAKE DEGREES AWARDED

Most diploma mills fish at the shallow end of the pool—the legal consequences of providing a fake high school diploma are probably minimal. Provide a fake medical degree, and you could end up as an accessory to murder.

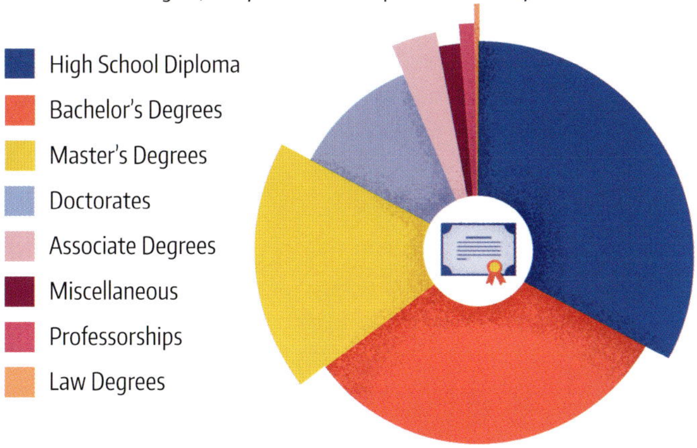

IS THAT ONLINE SCHOOL BEING JUST A LITTLE TOO PUSHY IN OFFERING ITS SERVICES? IF ITS REP SOUNDS MORE LIKE A HEAVY-HANDED SALESPERSON THAN AN EDUCATOR, YOU'RE PROBABLY DEALING WITH A DEGREE MILL.

KEY CONCEPT

WHAT YOU KNOW
One concept that questionable schools take advantage of is that of prior, or "life experience," learning. This can be a valid—if sometimes controversial or misused—tool. For example, let's say that an American student who takes four years of French at the university level can earn 24 credits. But what about a student who learns the language herself from online classes or while living in Paris? Many schools will give her some language-learning credit (although rarely that full 24 credits) once she's demonstrated her proficiency through written and oral exams. Some less-savory schools play to vanity by claiming that your life is so awesome that you've earned a degree just by living it! Or, more likely, that your years in business qualify you for an MBA with no extra study, something no legitimate school would suggest you do.

you send the check, we send the degree) or low (we just can't be bothered to fire up the printer).

LEARNING MORE ABOUT A SCHOOL Questions to ask would include: What is the size of the faculty? How many of these are full-time, part-time, and adjunct? Where did the faculty members earn their degrees? From which schools did the president, the dean, and other administrators earn theirs? While there's nothing wrong with faculty members earning degrees from their own school, once that number climbs to more than 25 percent, it starts sounding a little suspicious.

May I Have Contact Information for Some Recent Graduates? Ask for the names and email addresses of people who graduated in your field of study or who are in your local area. Most, but not all, reputable schools will supply this information.

May I Look at Some Coursework? An examination of master's theses and doctoral dissertations for the relevant degrees can often give a good idea of the quality of work expected of students and how well they rise to those expectations. Not every school will want to go through the hassle, or have obtained the proper permissions from students, but it's worth asking. Not everything is digitized; you may need to pay photocopying and shipping fees. Or visit the school—if you can afford to make the trip, it can be very revealing.

Will Your Degree Meet My Stated Needs? As noted earlier, there are several reasons you might seek a degree: state licensing or certification (for example, marriage therapy or primary education), requirements for graduate school admissions, qualifying for a new job, and so on. The school can't tell you with any authority whether the degree will get you a raise at your job or help you find a new one—and if it does, that's a red flag. But it should be able to speak to whether the degree will satisfy academic or professional requirements.

What Is Your Legal Status? If the school is located in the United States, ask about its status with both state and accrediting agencies. If it claims to be accredited, is it with an agency approved by the Department of Education or the Council for Higher Education Accreditation? If not, why? Does it plan to seek accreditation? If the school claims accreditation from a nation other than that where it is located, that's another red flag. Ask about this—usually it's because the accrediting nation has lax standards, but there could be a valid reason for the situation.

How Do You Handle Financial Aid? One of the necessary aspects of higher education in the United States is, of course, paying to enroll in the courses. If the college demands money up front, offers a pay-as-you-go system for its degree, or refuses to accept federal financial aid, these are serious warning signs to watch out for.

THE TAKEAWAY

Many totally legitimate and academically rigorous degree programs are offered online. So are a lot of worthless scams. Here's how to tell the difference..

BASIC SECURITY	• Check the school out in a reputable college directory. • Only deal with accredited universities—and don't take it on faith that they're accredited. Check. • If it sounds too good to be true, it probably is. If the only "work" required for your degree is giving them your credit card, be very skeptical.
ADVANCED MEASURES	• Ask to speak with graduates of the program you're interested in. • Ask if you can "audit" some online courses to assess the instruction and student engagement. • Scope it out on Google Earth.
TINFOIL-HAT BRIGADE	• Visit the school in person to check out their facilities. • If you can't travel to the location, see if you can hire a local through TaskRabbit or Craigslist to play private detective and snap some images of the buildings and grounds.

GOOD TO KNOW

ACCREDITATION
Standards and laws for accreditation vary by nation, state, or field. It's easy to say that a traditional university accredited by an official U.S. government–approved agency is the gold standard, but there are enough oddities, exceptions, and loopholes that things get confusing quickly.

In several nations, schools are authorized by national government ministries. Sometimes the process is rigorous, sometimes . . . less so. If academic integrity truly matters, check out those international schools carefully. If the school is somewhere unusual, ask plenty of questions.

In the United States, accrediting agencies are private companies that must gain recognition from the Department of Education after meeting fairly stringent standards. If a particular accrediting agency is not recognized, then you'll want to find out exactly why that is the case.

CHAPTER 4

INTERNET VIGILANTES AND MOB RULES

THE INTERNET HAS BROUGHT US CLOSER TO EACH OTHER—BUT TECHNOLOGY DOESN'T MAKE MANY PEOPLE NICER TO EACH OTHER. LEARN HOW TO PROTECT YOURSELF FROM ONLINE JERKS AND FROM EVEN BECOMING ONE YOURSELF.

Technology has connected us in a global village, but that doesn't mean we can always speak to each other civilly. According to a recent study by the Pew Research Center, 40 percent of adult internet users have experienced online harassment directly, and 73 percent have seen it happen. The technology that connects us to others around the world can be used to torment—both on- and offline. Welcome to the dark world of trolling, doxxing, anonymous ops, and online mobs.

The internet has decentralized everything, and harassment and mass protesting are no different. Online harassment can escalate to threats, prank calls to police departments, canceled speaking events, ruined careers—even driving some victims off the internet completely. Who are these trolls? Some want to entertain themselves, but the majority are bored teenagers who have turned to the internet to create their own drama, to get back at their friends, or win one-upmanship points. Having said that, the same technology can also be used for positive ends—stopping animal abuse, shutting down spammers, and protesting unfair internet laws.

Technology brings out the best and the worst in humanity. Learn how to protect yourself when the worst of humanity unleashes itself on the internet.

MEET YOUR INNER TROLL It used to be thought that mean people are born that way. But a new study from Stanford University suggests that, under the right conditions, anyone can be a troll.

The experiment exposed subjects to negative moods and/or comments and then asked participants to make their own comments. Those exposed to either the negative mood or comments were more likely to post negative statements; subjects exposed to both negative mood and comments were even more likely.

Negative comments can have serious emotional power—causing a downward spiral, with users returning to defend their statements and dig in their heels deeper. The negativity builds on itself and keeps growing. It's true: Just like laughter, trolling is contagious. Next time you're cranky and tempted to troll, pause, take a breath, then step away from the internet to cool off.

KEY CONCEPT

TROLLING The word "troll" conjures up images of a monstrous figure lurking under a bridge, but its origins are a different beast altogether. The word comes from the verb "to troll," which describes the fishing method of dragging a lure as bait. Internet trolls are similarly using "bait" when they post incendiary, hostile, and provocative information in order to lure others into having an argument with them. Trolls love to provoke people to get a reaction, and they also enjoy keeping the game going as long as possible, indulging in all of the anger and frustration they evoke. In internet-speak, lulz, derived from the slang term LOL (from "laugh out loud"), is laughter at the expense of others, a sort of modern schadenfreude. "Doing it for the lulz" means that trolls do what they do specifically so they can get an emotional rise out of their target.

BAD BEHAVIOR Trolling, harassment, and bullying create emotional distress and can lead to offline violence and real-world crimes, such as stalking or swatting. Trolls pop up in video game chats, review sites, on forums (especially 4chan, 7chan, and Reddit), and social media sites, including Twitter and Facebook. Trolls love all comment sections—in news stories and on YouTube, Tumblr, and even your blog if you've caught their attention. Companies have been trolled on Yelp, and individuals (including a White House spokesperson) have even been trolled on the payments platform Venmo. One thing is certain: Trolls are creative, and where they can troll, they will.

What They Do Online harassment includes sending nasty emails, sharing victims' personal information online, and calling for violence against targets. Many women even receive assault and death threats.

Stay Clear Trolls have no rules and will contradict themselves. They aren't logical, so don't bother trying to reason with them. They start arguments, post negative and shocking comments, give wrong information, and get people riled up. They're after angry reactions that keep the reprisals coming—they delight in creating chaos.

Trolls sometimes work together, posting targets in shared troll forums so that many of them go after the same target. These trolls get cred for participating in such ops.

GOOD TO KNOW

KNOW YOUR ENEMY Trolling takes a number of forms, including these common ones.

Dogpiling An internet cybermob descends on their target, trying to overwhelm, exhaust, and humiliate the victim.

Concern Trolling Someone gives "helpful" advice that's actually meant to belittle and demean the target.

Gaslighting The act of manipulating victims to make them doubt their own perception, memory, and sanity. If an abuser says it's not abuse, you are being gaslit.

Gish Galloping The objective in gish galloping involves a nonstop attempt to wear victims down, waste their time, and distract and sidetrack them. It's death by a thousand microcomments.

Impersonation Trolling As a way of discrediting targets, some trolls create fake social media accounts in their names and post provocative statements. Trolls might even take these false statements from the fake social media account and accuse the account holder of having made those statements.

Newbie Trolling There are always newcomers to online communities, and these folks can be taken advantage of by those sharing bad advice or giving misdirection.

Sea-Lioning These trolls join an online conversation and ask targets for their evidence. While generally civil, they question the facts and constantly challenge them—and then play the victim when their harassment is called out.

Shock Trolling Similar to radio DJ "shock jocks," these trolls go into a sensitive community (usually a religious or political forum) and stir up trouble by posting incendiary responses, images, or links.

HACKER HISTORY

ANONYMOUS ARISES
4chan, one of the most infamous forums on the internet, was started in 2003 by fifteen-year-old Christopher Poole. The notorious /b/ board, with an anarchic anything-goes attitude, is where many classic internet memes originated (such as Rickrolling and LOLcats) along with the hacktivist group Anonymous.

Legend says that Anonymous's first op was to save a cat from a teenage abuser who had posted YouTube videos of himself beating the animal. Forum members tracked down the poster, called the police, and had the cat rescued and the abuser arrested. The decentralized community went on to execute "ops" such as Project Chanology (targeting the Church of Scientology), DDoS attacks against other targets, and support of the Occupy movement. Anonymous derives its name from the anonymous nature of the 4chan /b/ board.

THE ONE THING TROLLS WANT FROM THEIR TARGETS IS A REACTION . . . ANY REACTION AT ALL. BY DENYING THEM THIS SATISFACTION, YOU MAY WELL MAKE YOURSELF A MUCH LESS ATTRACTIVE TARGET.

RANDOM ACTS OF TROLLING

It's theorized that the anonymity of the internet allows people to unleash their worst selves and hassle complete strangers. The facts as reported by victims of harassment online seem to bear this out.

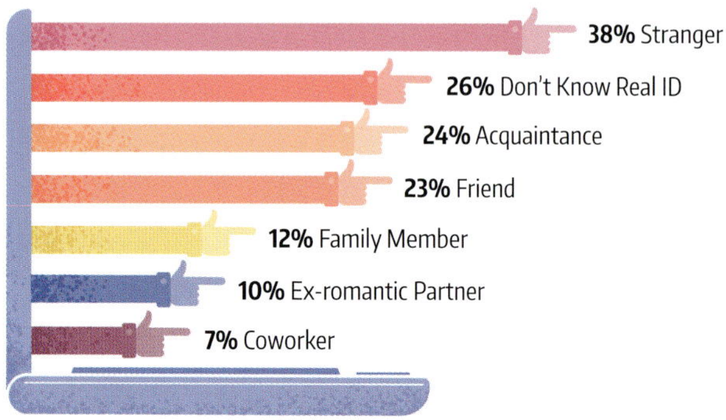

KEEP CALM AND CLICK ON Trolls poke at you in order to evoke an emotional reaction. The most important thing to remember is "don't feed the troll." Sure, it's hard to control yourself when someone is pushing all your buttons, but that's what the cyberbully is after. Stop a moment, take your hands away from the keyboard, take a breath, and get up and go for a walk. If you don't respond, the troll will get bored and go after an easier target.

Online communities have dealt with trolls from the beginning of the internet, and many have developed rules and software to keep trolls out. Soft banning is a technique that basically hides troll posts from everyone except the troll. If no one sees the post, it won't get attention, so the troll gets bored and goes elsewhere.

You can't predict whether you will be the target of online harassment. Women are typically harassed more than men, but anyone can be targeted for any reason, including political or religious beliefs. If you end up the victim of a troll or online harassment, here are some helpful responses.

Don't Engage Do not respond or show emotion when provoked. If you show the slightest reaction, they will go in for the kill. They can be relentless, and sometimes when they don't get a response, they will escalate further to provoke you into responding.

Document Everything Take screenshots of incendiary texts, tweets, and comments immediately, as they can be removed. Keep a harassment diary. If it's too upsetting for you to do it yourself, have a friend take over for you.

Protect Yourself Use strong passwords, and turn on two-factor authentication to make it harder to hack your accounts. Remove your personal information from the internet to make it harder to be doxxed (see "Key Concept," at right).

Take Legal Action Contact the appropriate authorities. Make a police report, although officers may not be able to help much unless the harassment goes outside the internet.

Vent Safely Trolls delight in upsetting people on the internet; responding or complaining online reads them. Instead of venting online, talk to a friend or family member you trust about your frustration or anger. Get some exercise, spend time with friends or loved ones, get out in nature, take care of yourself—eat well, drink water, and meditate to let the anger go. If it gets really stressful, seek the help of a professional.

Shut Them Out Unfriend, block, mute, and report trolls. Most systems have ways to block and report unsavory behavior—Twitter, YouTube, and Facebook, for example, all have block and reporting capabilities.

Give No Comment If you are posting an article or blog post that you think will be controversial, turn off comments. If a troll is responding to a blog post on your site or a Facebook post you started, you should feel free to turn off commenting midstream or to just delete the offending comment.

Disappear from Sight As a last-ditch option, consider creating a new identity for the forum or site on which you have been trolled.

KEY CONCEPT

DOXXING Short for "documenting," doxxing is when your personal information, such as your legal name, your address, phone number, email address, or other data is posted online—along with an open invitation for others to harass you. If people know your name and address, they can take harassment offline and it can get violent.

Prank calls to law enforcement about a false threat associated with a target's home is called "swatting." The goal here is to have armed police show up aiming guns at innocent people.

Swatting is illegal and can result in jail time. Notably, twenty-one-year-old Mir Islam, pleaded guilty to cyberstalking, doxxing, and swatting over fifty celebrities and public officials. He was sentenced to twenty-four months in prison. And after introducing the Interstate Swatting Hoax Act of 2015, Massachusetts Representative Katherine Clark became the victim of swatting.

GAMERGATE

THE INSTIGATORS AND SUPPORTERS OF GAMERGATE CLAIM THAT IT'S REALLY JUST ABOUT ETHICS IN GAMING JOURNALISM. BUT A LOOK A THE HISTORY OF GAMERGATE SHOWS THAT IT'S ABOUT FAR MORE AND FAR WORSE.

Gamergate started in 2014 with a blog post carefully crafted to rile up gangs of online trolls. As intended, it incited a serious cybermob trolling operation. The attacks got so out of control that they garnered media attention not just in the gamer community but in the mainstream as well. Gamergate was by no means the first major trolling op, but it was arguably one the most effective based on the number of on- and offline harassment attempts it spawned.

The seed that kicked off Gamergate was a nasty post written by Eron Gjoni, the spurned ex-boyfriend of game developer Zoe Quinn. They couple had dated for five months. After they broke up, Gjoni decided to harass Quinn to get back at her for the breakup. So he wrote a 9,425-word blog intended to get the gamer/troll audience to harass Quinn.

In aiming his blog post at the young, white, middle-class males who make up the vast majority of the gaming community, Gjoni was able to spur an organized attack—and not just on his ex-girlfriend. Mostly teens used to playing first-person shooter video games, these young men had begun to feel threatened by the growing diversity in the gaming field as more women and people of color started playing and making games, as well as criticizing existing games for their lack of diversity and their tendency to stereotype women as sex objects. Gjoni had hit a raw nerve in the white male–dominated gaming culture.

The post resulted in a firestorm of on- and offline

sexual harassment not just for Quinn but for scores of other women in the gaming community. Using the hashtag #GamerGate, trolls used the mask of philosophical disagreement to launch online attacks including negative comments and tweets, doxxing, disturbing Photoshopped images of the victims, inappropriate reports of the content they created, and assault and death threats. Anita Sarkeesian who produces Feminist Frequency, a website analyzing women's portrayal in pop culture, was another target. Brianna Wu, another developer, was doxxed and subsequently received death and rape threats. (Wu has gone on to start a legal defense fund and launched a campaign to run for Congress in 2018.) The same people who claimed they were focusing on "ethics" delivered bomb threats to organizations and conferences where any of their female targets were scheduled to speak or be given awards.

"QUINN WAS JUST THE FIRST WOMAN TARGETED."

The cybermob was relentless in its attempts to humiliate its victims, ruin their reputations, and destroy their peace of mind.

Gamergate was a perfect storm of online harassment, sexism, and immaturity. At its core, Gamergate has truly been about the online sexual harassment of women in the games industry. It caused untold emotional damage to its victims, while the perpetrators hid behind anonymous accounts. And it's not the first case of cybermob online sexual harassment, though its massive collective effort was notable. In an earlier case, Kathy Sierra, a prominent user experience expert, received similar harassment and threats, causing her to leave the internet in 2007.

Unfortunately, Gamergate won't be the last case, either. The internet is a perfect medium for anonymous harassment. Anyone can be a target, so take steps to protect yourself from trolls: Don't react to their posts, take screenshots of messages and images, report the incidents to authorities, and use strong passwords on social media accounts. Hopefully any trolls will slink away. But perhaps the best way to end online harassment is to not do it yourself—and to discourage others from trolling as well.

LESSON LEARNED

Gamergate was truly a watershed moment in the history of online trolling and sexual harassment. For the first time, an individual was able to strongly motivate and manipulate a sizable community to do his dirty work for him. Once the first rock was thrown, it kicked off an avalanche that was impossible to stop. Others joined in for the lulz, new targets were identified, and the mob swelled further in scale and behavior. Gamergate gained national media attention when the online harassment of its targets escalated to doxxing; rape and death threats; and threats of bombings, shootings, and other violent acts planned for conferences where the various women were booked as speakers. These techniques exploded during the alt-right media coverage of the 2016 election. And to think that this all started out with a jilted lover wanting revenge on his ex when he was ditched.

TROLLING GENERALLY ARISES FROM A COMBINATION OF BOREDOM, DISTANCE, ANONYMITY, AND OPPORTUNITY. MAKE SURE YOU DON'T SLIP INTO TROLLING OUT OF BOREDOM OR ANGER.

MOBS OR VIGILANTES? So far we have focused on the bad things that happen when people team up anonymously on the internet. That's not always the way it works. Technology is value-agnostic, and the same tools, techniques, and tendencies that have been used for evil have done a fair amount of good. Welcome to the world of hacktivism and decentralized political power, where anyone with a computer can be an activist, and where trolling can be used for justice or in protest of injustice.

Project Chanology We discussed earlier the way in which the group now known as Anonymous started out of the /b/ random forum on 4chan. And while much of those activities were for the lulz, there was an equal desire to use the power for good. Anonymous took on Scientology in 2008 when a leaked video of Tom Cruise promoting Scientology was removed from YouTube. The op was called Project Chanology. What followed were multiple DDoS attacks, black faxes (wherein an image of a black page is sent to the recipient's fax machine so as to use up as much toner as possible, causing cost and annoyance), and staged physical protests. Since Scientology is known to intimidate and harass protesters, Anonymous protesters wore masks to underscore their message: "We are Anonymous. We are Legion. We do not forgive. We do not forget. Expect us." The mask they chose, which have now become synonymous with the movement is the "Guy Fawkes" mask worn by anti-government protesters in the graphic novel and movie V for Vendetta.

Anonymous didn't stop with Scientology. Since the group is decentralized with no single leader, anyone can create an op, and anyone who wants to participate in the op joins. Anonymous has gone on to support to Occupy Wall Street and protest the KKK, ISIS, and the terrorists who conducted various attacks in Europe.

Trolling the Westboro Baptist Church The Westboro Baptist Church is known for its campaign of hate, displaying antigay signs at rallies and military funerals, as well as picketing and harassing other religions. After the church's leaders decided to turn its efforts toward harassing victims of the Sandy Hook school mass shooting in 2012, Anonymous focused its efforts on them. The Westboro Baptist Church website was quickly hacked and shut down, the social media accounts of several of its members were likewise compromised, and a charge was led in petitioning the government to declare the church a hate group.

Chasing Child Molesters In 2007, Canadian citizen Chris Forcand was arrested on multiple counts of soliciting a minor after several members of Anonymous engaged with him online pretending to be minors and collecting logs of the chats and inappropriate photos he sent. In 2011, Anonymous's efforts went further with Operation Darknet, whereby the group targeted and brought down forty hidden sites run by internet provider Freedom Hosting—all of them soliciting inappropriate content—and releasing the names of more than 1,500 users to the general public. In 2015, Operation Death Eater emerged, which is an effort to combat international pedophile groups.

Grassroots Advocacy Along with its larger-scale ops, Anonymous has also engaged in several smaller-scale or less-well-known activities, such as Operation Beast, which has targeted sites engaging in animal abuse; Operation Monsanto, which focuses on protests against the agriculture corporation; and Operation Safe Winter, a campaign working to create awareness of the difficulties faced by homeless people during cold winter months.

KEY CONCEPT

HACKTIVISM The internet has provided new opportunities for people to connect with each other—although not always in the best of ways—and one of those opportunities has been the ability to participate in social and political activism without having to leave one's home. Reputedly coined in 1994 by a member of the hacker group called the Cult of the Dead Cow, hacktivism is a combination of "hacking" and "activism" rooted in hacker culture and ethics. Those who are dedicated to a cause can use the internet in a subversive manner to promote social or political change. Most often the desire is to spread information and push for civil and human rights. Of course, due to the less-than-savory ways in which some have abused the internet, hacktivism has also had its unpleasant aspects, such as the Gamergate phenomenon (see pages 46–47 for more).

SECURITY BASIC

STAYING UNDER THE RADAR Do you know if your personal information—like your full legal name and your home address—is available online? Many sites have made a business model making this kind of information public. Others are looking to make it easy to create family trees. And on some sites, your information comes up with a simple search. Recently passed laws, however, require these sites to remove you from their databases if you request to opt out. Of course, there are companies, such as DeleteMe, looking to make a profit by doing this automatically for you. The reason you might want to remove your data from these databases is because this is where trolls get the information to doxx you and bring online harassment offline. Make it harder for trolls to find your information by removing as much of it as you can now.

MEET YOUR INNER TROLL

Everyone has a little bit of a dark side, and trolling can bring out the worst in our natures. Here are some of the personality factors that make a troll.

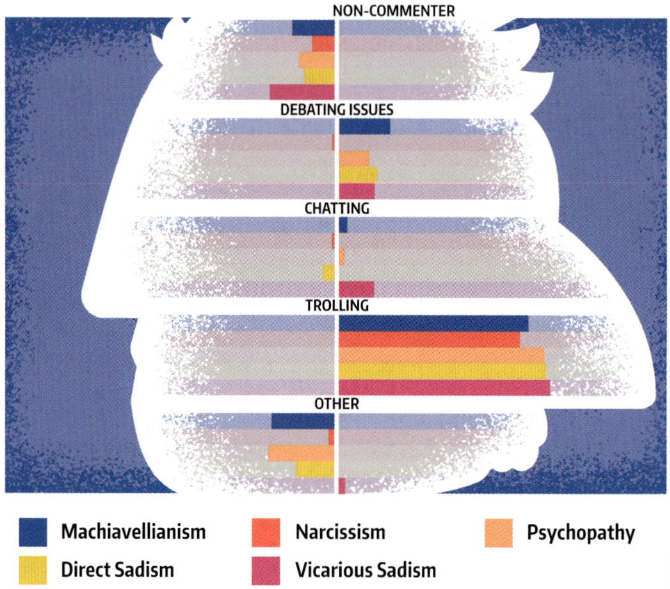

WHAT MAKES A TROLL? Just as there will always be some unpleasant or troublesome people in society, ultimately the same is true on the internet. Trolling is unlikely to ever truly go away until humanity itself changes. A combination of distance, anonymity, and opportunity are a temptation that can sometimes bring out the worst in others, giving rise to their inner troll. But there may be a higher predisposition in some people. Psychological studies on sociopathy and antisocial behavior have presented the concept of the dark triad, a combination of three personality characteristics, that when combined, paint a dark picture of a malevolent individual.

The nefarious traits that are referred to by the dark triad are Machiavellianism, narcissistic behavior, and psychopathy, which, when combined, create a personality that has low empathy, a thrill-seeking nature, enjoys manipulating other people, and is focused on ego gratification. If you compare this to the activities of trolls—causing distress, doing it for the lulz, seeing victims as their source of entertainment, and "operations"—you can see how trolls fit this description. Given the opportunity, anyone has the potential to be a troll—but there are some people who may be born for it.

Remember the Good All this talk of trolls, vigilantes, 4chan, Anonymous, and Gamergate can of course paint a bleak picture that the internet is a foreboding place filled with potentially hostile figures waiting to bully or harass you for their own entertainment. But you should still keep in mind that there are also a lot of good people doing good things on the internet. By taking measures to avoid becoming a victim of trolling—and not becoming a troll yourself—you can guarantee that there will always be more good people than bad on the internet.—Heather Vescent

THE TAKEAWAY

Don't let your internet experience be ruined by a bunch of creepy kids and sad puppies. Here's how to avoid trolls or, if the worst happens, deal with them deftly.

BASIC SECURITY	• Block, mute, hide, and unsubscribe from troublemakers. • Stay away from the comments section below online articles. • Step away from social media if you start getting too worked up. • Don't take even the worst attacks personally.
ADVANCED MEASURES	• Lock down the privacy settings on all social media. • Use two-factor authentication for all accounts. • Ask site admins if comments are moderated and stay away from any sites where they're not.
TINFOIL-HAT BRIGADE	• Only post under a pseudonym; don't use your real name for any social media or forums. • Create an email account you only use for social media (or other high-risk functions, such as online dating or gaming). Make the name nothing like your own and don't link it to anything else. • Document online harassment and take it to the police.

GOOD TO KNOW

DOING TROLLING RIGHT We can't, in all good conscience, actually tell you to go out there and troll others when you get bored. But we do know there are some people who can't resist the urge. But you should really know what you're getting into if you're going to let your inner troll out. If you're going to troll, do so with class. Use wit and refined thought as much as possible to point out the issue you've taken exception to. Pick a proper target—this means, as they say in comedy circles, "punching up." Choose an organization that has been problematic or harmful to innocent victims rather than belittling someone smaller and weaker ("punching down"). And always, always, be prepared for backlash. People out there will eventually decide they don't like how you've expressed yourself. Hey, we never said trolling was easy.

HACK THE WORLD

It wasn't too long ago that politicians and pundits were referring to the internet as our era's answer to the old Wild West—a lawless new frontier where fortunes could be made and reputations ruined. And the fact is, even if most internet searches are for cat videos and muffin recipes, plenty of sketchy stuff is still going on in the darker corners of cyberspace. Those shady back alleys provide shelter for good guys and bad from whistleblowers, political dissidents, and those who leak secret documents to cyberspies, drug dealers, and global terrorists. Whether you're looking to bring down an oppressive regime or learn how to crash a nation's infrastructure, there's someone out there who's interested in helping. Can you trust them? Probably not. Read on before saddling up and heading off to conquer this new frontier.

CHAPTER 5

THE DEEP DARK NET

YOU MAY HAVE HEARD MENTION OF THE DARKNET ON COP SHOWS OR IN NEWS STORIES ABOUT GUNS, DRUGS, AND MURDER FOR HIRE. IS IT REALLY SO DARK OUR THERE? SOMETIME IT IS—BUT NOT ALWAYS. LET'S GO FOR A DIVE AND SEE.

Aside from their rather evocative (and nearly meaningless) monikers, few people actually know what the "deep web" and "darknet" are—or understand the differences between the two. In this chapter, we'll look at what happens when you venture away from the brightly lit thoroughfares of the information superhighway and explore some of its shadier back alleyways. While in reality it's neither as glamorous nor as murderous as various crime shows on TV make it out to be, the fact remains that this aspect of the internet is a significant contributor to the world's economy—and to global criminal activity as well.

Although we can assume that a large number of the transactions on the darknet are relatively benign (although that depends on whether you consider stolen Netflix logins or off-brand Viagra to be harmless), many are not. As with any lawless wild frontier, you can find some real bad guys profiting off humanity's darker side. In this case, those bad guys might be dealing drugs or selling hacked credit card accounts. That said, some of the good guys out there can benefit from the same anonymity as well, particularly if they happen to be whistleblowers or individuals fighting oppressive regimes.

SHADY DEALINGS How much money is changing hands out there on the so-called darknet? More than you might think, although by their very nature, these sorts of transactions are obviously difficult to track and quantify. Reliable experts estimate that black-market transactions account for about 23 percent of the world's total goods and services. Think about that. If the global world product is almost $78 trillion USD, that means almost $18 trillion more is traded through the black market. In other words, almost a quarter of the world's transactions occur outside of the legitimate global exchanges. What are those transactions? Anyone who wants to make or receive untraceable (and untaxed) payments for anything, including illegal goods and services—from guns and drugs to hacking and stolen data—can find what they are looking for on the digital black market.

KEY CONCEPT

A PRIVATE PLACE
Not everything on the darknet is illegal. In fact, it was originally designed by the U.S. government to let their operatives and analysts anonymously explore the farthest reaches of the global internet, in search of information. Privacy and anonymity are paramount to all users of the darknet, and many use it simply because they can communicate free from fear of online surveillance. Consider life in some countries where freedom of expression is not a right. Learning about, for example, government abuses by accessing foreign websites blocked by your nation is now safely possible using the darknet, as is expressing hopes and dreams—and, yes, buying a pair of counterfeit Versace sunglasses. When you consider the arbitrary nature of laws being an extension of the arbitrary power of government, the beauty of the darknet is clear.

GOING DEEPER The first thing to know in getting your head around this topic is that the web is not the internet. While they may seem synonymous in daily life, the internet is far more than the World Wide Web. The internet is the entire global set of computers connected to a giant public network that shares certain rules for communicating various types of information. The most familiar of these are web pages and emails, but there are in fact many other things you'd never notice or care about that run over this same global network. Here's the basic breakdown.

The Surface Web Most of what you see online, from Facebook to eBay to Amazon to Twitter, is the surface web. It's made up of all the various public websites that share content, sell goods, or otherwise want to be easily found. They allow any guest to visit, and they invite search engines to index them so that users can find them through Google, Yahoo, and the like.

The Deep Web Millions of sites out there don't appear in search engines, often because they don't want to be found easily. These sites have no inbound links from any other site, and they block search engines. You can still visit them using a standard browser, but only if you have some other way of knowing the address, for example, if a link is sent in private email to a specific list of recipients. This type of arrangement is often used to share content, such as hacked data, with a closed community that wants no outsiders.

The Darknet Simply put, the "darknet" is anything that cannot be accessed via a standard browser because it requires special software, and often special knowledge, to access. The darknet typically refers to sites on the Tor network (more on that on page 60) that look and feel just like regular sites but require a special Tor browser to view. The darknet, more broadly, includes other protocols and environments common users don't know about, such as IRC (internet relay chat) channels and I2P (Invisible Internet Project) networks. In addition, the darknet isn't indexed the way surface web sites are; virtually all of its sites' addresses must be shared instead of searched for, and not everyone out there will be keen on sharing.

The bottom line is that, for average users, the deep and dark web may seem alluring or sexy thanks to television. In reality, what you'll find there is malware, viruses, illegal content, and criminals ready to take advantage of the uninitiated. Unless you really know what you're doing, keep out.

KEY CONCEPT

SHOPPING IN THE DARK While it offers many legitimate uses to activists, whistleblowers, law enforcement, and political refugees, the darknet also supports an underground black-market economy that follows its own set of rules. Buyers and sellers have many reasons to trade outside normal open markets. These can include the following.

Illegal Goods Anyone looking for products or services that can't be sold in the open, such as drugs, stolen identity data, or weapons.

Anonymity These transactions can be done without records, allowing the buyer and seller to remain anonymous, with (theoretically) no paper trail or electronic footprint.

Price Controls Products that are subject to taxation, import duties, price controls, and other constraints—such as cigarettes or alcohol—are attractive to black-market profiteers. So are products such as Tide laundry detergent, Gillette Mach3 razors, Crest whitening strips, and other huge-markup common necessities.

Technology has made it easier for black-market buyers and sellers to safely connect and do business. In the constant back-and-forth between authorities and black markets, one black market is shut down, but another takes its place.

T/F

YOU CAN HIRE A HITMAN ON THE INTERNET

TRUE The most notorious online black market was Silk Road, operated by a hacker known as the Dread Pirate Roberts in 2011. It was an online marketplace functioning much like eBay or Amazon, except the offerings included guns, illegal drugs, hacking services, and even murder for hire. Silk Road was shut down by the FBI in November 2013, and Ross William Ulbricht, the Dread Pirate Roberts, is now serving a lifetime prison sentence. Not surprisingly, countless other illicit marketplaces have sprung up in its place. It's not entirely clear whether the many "hit for hire" services are pure fantasy or con men preying on the gullible. On the other hand, if they were as good as they say, how would we know?

IF YOU DO DECIDE TO GO EXPLORING THE DARKNET, DISABLE ALL SCRIPTS IN YOUR BROWSER. YOU NEVER KNOW WHAT MALWARE OUT THERE COULD BE CAPABLE OF ATTACKING YOUR COMPUTER.

PEELING AWAY THE ONION The largest and best-known element of the darknet is the Tor network. Tor, which stands for "The Onion Router," was originally a project started by the U.S. Navy but has long since been turned over to a private nonprofit organization. The details are extremely technical, but, as an average user, you can think of the Tor network as three related technologies.

A Web Browser The Tor browser works like a normal web browser, but it routes users requests for web pages through the Tor network.

Safe Passage Tor anonymizes users' activity by stripping identifying data from page requests, then sending the requests through multiple encrypted transfers between volunteer-run computers all over the world that run special Tor software, letting them act as transit points. When a user with a Tor browser types in a standard web address, that request goes from the "normal" web into Tor, gets bounced through various intermediate relays, then reenters the normal web via a Tor "exit node" and arrives at the destination website. The site responds to the page request, and the content is sent back to the user by the Tor network through a similar process.

Hidden Websites Computers equipped with the right Tor software can also run websites (and other services, including IRC chat channels) accessible a via Tor browser. So users with a Tor browser are able to not only anonymize their browsing of the standard web but can see a whole second "web" (albeit relatively small) made up of sites ending in .ONION that can't be reached by a standard browser.

Software for browsing acting as a node or hosting a Tor website can be found at TORproject.org.

PEELING THE ONION

Using Tor means that internet traffic on the browser is routed through multiple layers of Tor user relays, like an onion—hence its name.

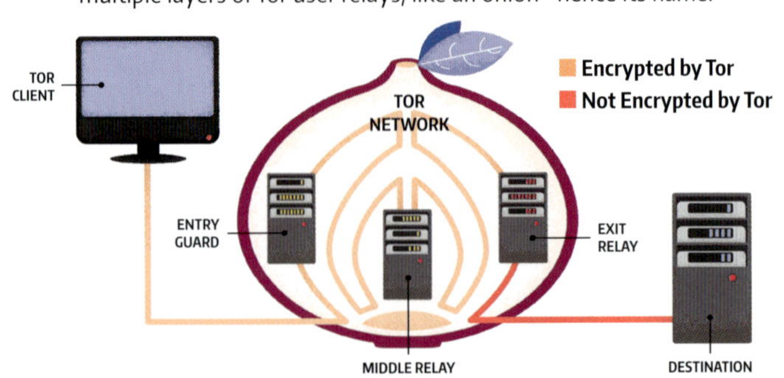

UNDERCOVER OPS While criminals lurk in the shadowy recesses of the darknet, so too do law enforcement officers from around the world. A colleague in the UK complained that he'd bought too many knives and drugs to know what to do with. I spend countless hours surfing Tor sites looking for producers of illegal goods (distinct from distributors, who are often careless enough to use the surface web to exchange their goods).

Shopping for Trouble The intrepid cyber security reporter Brian Krebs has taken on so many darknet criminals that his local police department had to come up with a special procedure when someone calls to report a violent crime at Krebs's house after SWAT teams, alerted by darknet thugs that there was a "hostage situation," had converged several times on his house. Krebs has also had criminals send heroin to his house, and then call authorities with the tip to search his mail.

"The darknet is where the bad guys are," a high-ranking federal agent told me. "We've got to get good at being there and looking like we belong there, because that's the only way we get into the kinds of conversations and relationships that will enable us to get leads and stop plots."

Reputation Matters This raises an important non-obvious point: In a world of anonymous users, reputation—based on common interests and sustained, consistent activity—is the only measure of trustworthiness. That's something that keeps academics busy.

Of course, reputation is how good reporters and journalists arrange to meet with sources to safely learn of corruption schemes and criminal gangs. The work done by these journalists is important in helping law enforcement and academic researchers understand new trends, and reporters can sometimes break stories based on darknet trading patterns. Brian Krebs, for example, broke the Target hack. Steve Ragan, another cyber reporter, has for years reported on criminal malware and hacktivist groups.

Check It Out—Carefully Who else is on the darknet? The morbidly curious—those who want to see whether you really can buy heroin and speed (you can) or hire a hit man (you can). The authors recommend you have a look around, if only to see for yourself the kinds of wares (and warez, aka pirated software) for sale, to educate yourselves about how the rest of this book isn't a bunch of people making stuff up. On the darknet, no one knows if you're a dog, but they do know if you have bitcoin (more on this digital currency in a bit).

FUN FACTS

WEIRD WARES The darknet may be a place to find guns, drugs, and hit men, but here are some of the stranger things you can buy on the DL.

Fake Coupons Grocers and snack companies have lost millions on everything from discounted cereal to free bags of chips.

Social Media Followers Wanna feel popular? For the low price of $25 USD, you can get 2,500 "followers" on Twitter.

Immortality You too can learn how to live forever! As long as you believe what the people selling the formula tell you.

Original Red Bull The energy drink now found worldwide was adapted from a more . . . potent formula originally sold in Thailand.

A New Identity Want to disappear? There are lots of guides on changing your identity. Plastic surgery not included.

THE DARKNET

144,000

TOTAL AMOUNT OF BITCOINS THE FBI SEIZED FROM ROSS ULBRICHT, THE ORIGINAL "DREAD PIRATE ROBERTS," FOUNDER OF SILK ROAD.

$12 MILLION

ESTIMATED VALUE OF BITCOINS LOST IN A "HEIST" WHEN THE EVOLUTION MARKET DISAPPEARED FROM THE DARKNET OVERNIGHT.

$100 MILLION

VALUE OF BITCOINS LOST WHEN SHEEP MARKETPLACE SHUT DOWN IN 2013, SCAMMING ITS MEMBERS.

$820K

VALUE OF BITCOINS THAT A FORMER SECRET SERVICE AGENT ADMITTED TO STEALING DURING THE SILK ROAD INVESTIGATION.

HERE'S A TIMELINE OF BITCOIN VALUE AT THE START OF EACH YEAR

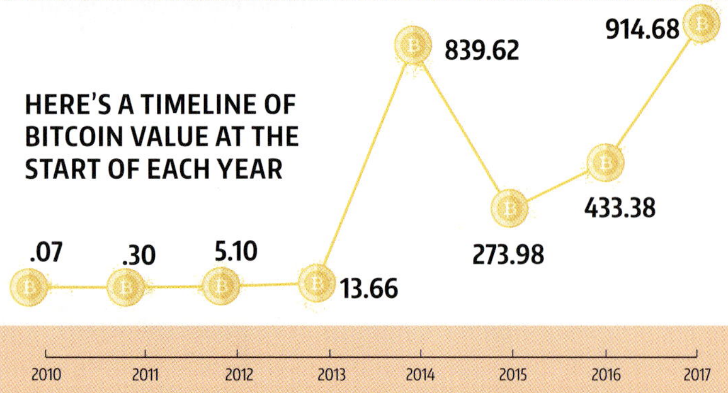

BITCOIN VALUES HAVE FLUCTUATED BETWEEN $0.0001 AND $1,250.99 IN ITS LIFETIME THUS FAR.

30,000 UNIQUE SITES OR SERVICES (MAKING UP ABOUT 350,000 WEB PAGES) CAN BE FOUND ON THE DARKNET.

HERE'S AN ESTIMATE OF WHAT THEY CONTAIN.

- **47.7%** DEAD SITES
- **19.6%** OTHER NON-ILLICIT USES
- **8.1%** DRUGS
- **6.3%** FINANCIAL FRAUD
- **1.8%** HACKING TOOLS
- **2.7%** POLITICAL EXTREMISM
- **2.3%** ILLEGAL PORN
- **1.1%** GUNS AND VIOLENCE
- **2.3%** DARKNET-BASED SEARCH ENGINES
- **3%** UNKNOWN
- **1.2%** SOCIAL SITES

3.4%

PERCENTAGE OF TRAFFIC THROUGH TOR USED FOR DARKNET ACTIVITY.

60 SECONDS

AMOUNT OF TIME IT TAKES TO SET UP A DARKNET BLACK-MARKET WEBSITE, USING STARTUP SOFTWARE DEEPIFY.

49

ESTIMATE NUMBER OF BLACK-MARKET WEBSITES CURRENTLY ACTIVE ON THE DARKNET.

$21.35 USD

AVERAGE COST FOR A NEW IDENTITY CARD

20%

ESTIMATED FRACTION OF ALL WORLDWIDE DRUG SALES THROUGH DARKNET MARKETS IN 2014.

$1.2 BILLION

ESTIMATED AMOUNT OF MONEY MADE THROUGH SILK ROAD DURING ITS 28 MONTHS OF OPERATION.

TRUE STORY

DREAD PIRATE ROBERTS AND SILK ROAD

BITCOIN + EBAY-LIKE BLACK MARKETPLACE + AMATEUR TECHIE + VISIONS OF CHALLENGING THE U.S. GOVERNMENT = SILK ROAD. A STORY AS SHADY AS THE DARK MARKET.

The internet has enabled new business models that connect buyers and sellers from around the world for illegal transactions as well as legal ones. eBay was one of the first big online marketplaces, and it has carefully policed sellers to be sure no one is breaking the law. So where's an online shopper looking for something a little less conventional to go? It was only a matter of time before something arose to serve those interests.

The breakthrough for illicit online marketplaces came when bitcoin, a decentralized digital currency that works a lot like cash, was introduced. Word on the street was that bitcoin allowed you to make purchases online with perfect anonymity. This turned out not to be the case, but it's still a more stealthy way to operate than, say, using PayPal to purchase that shoulder-mounted grenade launcher you've had your eye on.

The first of the darknet markets, Silk Road was started in February 2011 by an anonymous self-taught administrator who later became known as the Dread Pirate Roberts, aka DPR. At the peak of Silk Road's popularity, it was estimated that the operation was bringing in $10K–$13K USD a month.

Silk Road emerged at a perfect time. It was like eBay but for black-market goods—mostly drugs, both illicit and pharmaceutical. As with eBay listings, sellers were rated, and there was an escrow to increase trust in the transactions.

There were certain illicit goods that were prohibited. DPR's philosophy was to hurt no one—thus stolen data was not allowed. DPR saw Silk Road as a new brand that would challenge the government status quo.

In June 2011, Silk Road got major press on a number of tech blogs. This attracted more users—and also the attention of law enforcement agencies.

Task forces from the FBI and the DEA were formed to unmask and take down DPR. One DEA agent, Carl Mark Force IV, donned an alternate identity—that of a mid-level drug cartel player from the Dominican Republic—and reached out to DPR. They struck up a genuine friendship, but it was complicated because Force, as a member of the Baltimore Silk Road Task Force, was still trying to bring DPR in.

"IT WAS LIKE EBAY BUT FOR BLACK-MARKET GOODS."

At one point, DPR asked Force to help him arrange the murder with DPR of a Silk Road employee who was cooperating with federal authorities. The task force managed to stage a convincing fake murder for hire.

The Silk Road bust came after months of chasing IP addresses and confirming site logins to DPR's account.

Chris Tarbell was the agent who eventually found Silk Road's IP address and traced it to a data center in Iceland. With a letter from the U.S. attorney, he walked out of the data center with a mirror of the drive, which was used to trace an IP address to Café Luna in San Francisco.

Ross William Ulbricht was the man arrested in October 2013 in San Francisco's Glen Park Public Library. All the bitcoins that were held on Silk Road servers were seized by the U.S. government and later sold in a series of auctions. Ulbricht was convicted of money laundering, computer hacking, and procuring murder. He is serving a life sentence without parole.

In a strange twist to the story, the undercover DEA agent Carl Force went rogue and was convicted of embezzling a small fortune of the seized bitcoins. He was sentenced to six and a half years in June 2015, including counts on money laundering and obstruction of justice. His colleague, Shaun Bridges, a former secret service agent, was also charged.

The Silk Road brand lives on, but it isn't controlled by Ulbricht. As of this printing, they're on Silk Road 3.0.

LESSON LEARNED

DARKNETS ALL THE WAY DOWN There have always been black markets, and they will never go away. Silk Road and the many sites that sprung up after its fall made buying illegal goods easy. As these sites became more popular, they also drew the eye of government. These black markets are lucrative, but most operators know they will eventually be busted. Buyers and sellers know this too and therefore keep minimal funds on the sites, in case they are seized. Criminals are both clever and greedy, and it seems like every new technology can be bent to nefarious uses. More tech-savvy criminals arise all the time, competing with laws and law enforcement—both sides aided by technology, which is itself value-agnostic. But how bad might it be, really, to have a clean, well-lit place for illicit transactions? For knowing the quality of the products sold? Some might say "Better the devil you know . . ."

SECURITY BASIC

KEEP YOUR IDENTITY OFF THE DARKNET

With the increasing numbers of site hacks, it's just a matter of time before your personal data is sold on the black market. There's not much you can do to protect yourself from someone else's site getting hacked—that's up to the site's security technology. But you can use good account password hygiene. Never reuse the same username/password combination on different sites. One of the first things hackers will do with freshly hacked data is automatically check the hacked username/password combos on numerous banking, social, and email websites. If you use the same username and password combination at other sites, hackers could get into your accounts on those sites, even though those sites were not hacked. Use a complex but easy to remember password combination.

LET THE BUYER BEWARE Until recently, the U.S. dollar, in cash, was the preferred currency for black-market transactions. Cash is untraceable and anonymous, but it's difficult to use cash for online commerce. Credit cards and other common payment methods leave a paper trail. That's why bitcoin is so ideal for shady shoppers. While as noted above they're not entirely anonymous, the use of bitcoin "tumblers" and anonymizing sites can obscure ones trail pretty well. Should you do this? There are legitimate reason to keep a light financial footprint, particularly if you subscribe to any number of concerns (or conspiracy theories, to unbelievers) about your government and its nosy ways.

Give It a (Careful) Go There are some reasons why a noncriminal user might consider these underground markets. For example, you might wish to rent access to the internet via another user's computer elsewhere in the world where, for example, Netflix shows first-run films not available to U.S. users, or you reside in a part of the world where freedom of expression is limited and you want to be able to communicate with others about civil rights or human rights issues.

Approach with Caution Small mistakes in your "operational security" can have massive consequences. It's not enough to be careful. You must be *very* careful and follow a strict set of procedures every time you enter and leave the darknet and even the deep web.

First off, don't use your own computer for this kind of exploration. In fact, you shouldn't even use a real-world one. Instead, download a bootable Linux image and always be sure to load your Tor sessions through that path. You should also load tools such as PGP (Pretty Good Privacy) encryption onto that bootable drive.

This setup will allow you to load your entire browsing session in the host computer's memory so that, when you finish, you restart the computer and there are no traces of the activity on your hard drive.

We don't recommend doing any shopping of course, but if you do get curious, don't just use Tor to access darknet sites. For extra anonymity, you'll want to use an additional VPN (virtual private network) to completely anonymize your traffic.

All these techno-stealth measures may seem like a lot of work, but they're really the only way to access the darknet with any degree of security. And that's important once you think about the fact that almost everyone who gets caught doing something illicit gets caught because of security lapses. We will even go so far as to recommend using a clean laptop—completely devoid of any personal data or links to legitimate online accounts such as banking—and thus dedicated only to your deep web and darknet adventures. You certainly don't want to be playing around in these neighborhoods with a computer that, if breached, would reveal a lot about your activities.

THE TAKEAWAY

The darknet is a fascinating place to spend a little time exploring, but dangers lurk everywhere, even if you're not doing anything illicit. Take reasonable precautions.

BASIC SECURITY

- Don't engage in any kind of illegal or questionable activity on the Internet.
- If you do any transactions on darknet sites, even perfectly legal ones, use encryption for everything.
- Disable all scripts ion your browser before logging on to Tor.

ADVANCED MEASURES

- Only use cryptocurrency for darknet transactions, and employ a tumbler to ensure optimal anonymity.
- Change usernames and passwords frequently.

TINFOIL-HAT BRIGADE

- Minimize coin kept in escrow to avoid losing it in a bust or heist.
- Use both Tor and a VPN to completely anonymize your traffic.
- Keep your data on a thumb drive so that you can erase all traces from your regular machine.

GOOD TO KNOW

THE FUTURE OF THE DARKNET Since the darknet has come into being, multiple changes have already taken place, and things will continue to change. Specific marketplaces will come and go—they're never going to go away entirely. Regulatory changes may influence what is sold on the black market, and some goods (such as marijuana, in places where it has been legalized) may transition to white markets. So what might we find on future black markets? In short: anything that is unregulated or highly regulated. This could be technology and drugs to augment the human body, government secrets, or new types of personal data, such as medical data collected by new consumer devices or household sensors. One thing is for certain: Future systems will be more secure than the ones that we have today—but future hackers will be more sophisticated as well.

CHAPTER 6

WIKILEAKS AND WHISTLEBLOWERS

SOMETIMES WHEN CONFIDENTIAL INFORMATION IS LEAKED TO THE PRESS IT'S TO SERVE THE GREATER GOOD. SOMETIMES IT'S A DISASTER FOR HEALTH AND SAFETY. THE PROBLEM IS TELLING WHICH IS WHICH WHEN SECRETS SHOW UP ONLINE.

The internet allows all sorts of operatives and opportunities to get access to treasure troves of data that would have been unimaginable back in the days of Watergate, when actual burglars had to break into a bricks and mortar hotel to lift a few measly documents. These days, millions of pages of classified records can be liberated with a little stealth and skill.

This means that it's easier than ever for legitimate government agencies (or of course jack-booted thugs, depending on your perspective) to obtain all kinds of information from voice and written communications surveillance. This type of intelligence gathering traditionally falls into the realm of what is known as signals intelligence, or SIGINT. Our national intelligence agencies concerned with the capture and analysis of SIGINT have never had such an advantage, and they have risen to the task.

The flip side? What's good for the goose has turned out to be far better for the gander who wants to steal that SIGINT. This affects governments trying to protect information as well as businesses that are vulnerable to corporate and industrial espionage Ultimately "Information wants to be free," as the saying goes . . . but at what price?

TRAITORS AND SCOUNDRELS In 1971, Daniel Ellsberg and Anthony Russo gave what became known as the "Pentagon Papers" to the *New York Times*. Ellsberg became that era's most celebrated (and/or despised) figure. The papers proved that presidents from Truman to Johnson lied about American involvement in Vietnam—and that Johnson had been bombing in secret. When the *Times* published, Ellsberg was heralded as a hero by antiwar protesters and excoriated as a traitor by those in government. This precedent set the stage for the WikiLeaks and Snowden affairs—among them, the understanding that newspapers can publish classified documents delivered to them (the Nixon administration had tried, in spectacularly poor fashion, to block publication), so long as they don't actively solicit their theft.

KEY CONCEPT

THE SECURITY TRIAD The guiding principle of the security field is that you need three factors to ensure a secure system.

Confidentiality You simply must know that data stored on your system is protected against unintended or unauthorized access. That certainty is immensely complex to implement since, for example, Chelsea Manning (see page 71) was authorized to access—but not to copy and share—files.

Integrity The data's consistency, accuracy, and trustworthiness must be maintained over its entire life cycle, with contingencies for human error, server crashes, and viruses.

Availability The best data in the world is useless if you can't consistently and reliably access it, no matter what technology you're using.

WIKILEAKS AND SIMILAR SITES In the last several years, mentions of WikiLeaks and other associated websites and individuals have become more and more prevalent in media and conversations about security. But some people may still be a bit fuzzy on just who they are and what they do.

What Are They? WikiLeaks—as well as its wiser, more mature, and, from a policy perspective, more lastingly impactful older brother, Cryptome (as well as thousands of similar sites that have sprung up around the world from time to time)—provide varying levels of anonymity to those willing to disclose to the public information or data that they feel is of interest. This information can range from government documents (such as intelligence reports,diplomatic communiqués, program outlines, and planning descriptions), to insider stock trading records. Other examples include logs of computer network breaches, inside corporate policy documents not intended for public consumption (for example, internal pricing or policies on pharmaceutical distribution), customer records (such as the private customer data leaked by the hacker collective Anonymous on customers—including me—of the private intelligence firm Stratfor), and anything else considered interesting.

Why Do They Exist? Reporters, muckrakers, short-sellers, investigators, opposition researchers, and suspicious spouses have always looked to insiders for these kinds of disclosures. The internet has simply made them easier to find.

What's Useful About Them? It can be argued quite well—and I do argue it—that our founding fathers had a hearty and healthy distrust of government, and they empowered the people to foment regularly this distrust through a vigorous and free press. If you believe that assertion, then you simply must believe that anything that empowers such a free press is, by definition, "useful." Regardless of your position on Edward Snowden, WikiLeaks, Chelsea Manning, or Daniel Ellsberg, that they are a part of public debate and discourse is ultimately better than why they are not.

What's the Downside? It is my personal belief that the kind of leaks inspired by Julian Assange—and committed by Chelsea Manning and especially by Edward Snowden—ultimately do more harm than good. When leaking is relatively easy (provided of course you have the access and the know-how), the kinds of thought and agonizing put into "what to leak" and "whether to leak it" exhibited by an Ellsberg or a Russo give way to the immediacy and the instant global celebrity attendant with the act of leaking, as we saw with the way Snowden gathered and disseminated some potentially deadly intelligence.

SURVEILLANCE AND SECURITY

Snowden leaked as many as 1.7 documents on a wide range of NSA operations, far more than we could ever describe here. Just as a small sampling, here are 10 notable things we learned that the NSA did.

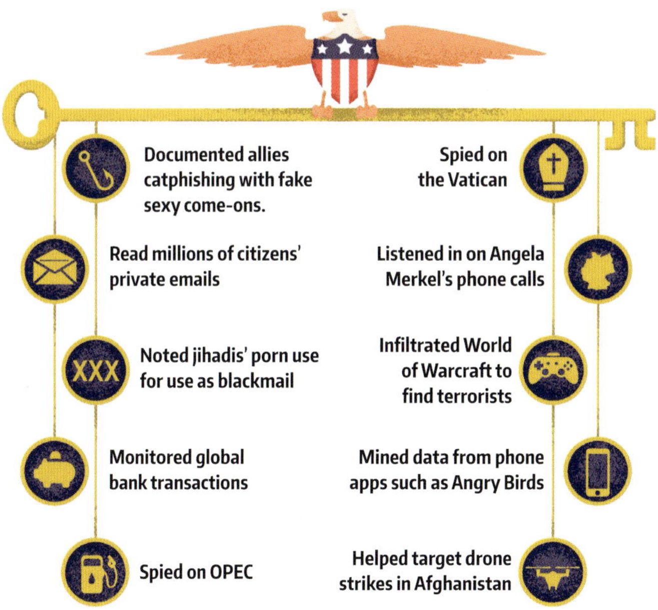

KEY PLAYER

CHELSEA MANNING

Born Bradley Manning (she began transitioning in government custody), Chelsea Manning was key to the first major WikiLeaks disclosure. As a soldier she was assigned in 2009 to an army unit in Iraq as an intelligence analyst. She had access to large amounts of confidential information and, in 2010, leaked more than 700,000 classified Iraq and Afghanistan war logs and diplomatic cables to Julian Assange of WikiLeaks. She said that she meant to do good by exposing military corruption and incompetence. In 2013, Manning was convicted of six espionage act violations as well as theft and computer fraud, and sentenced to thirty-five years in jail. She was acquitted of aiding the enemy, which carries a possible death sentence. In 2017, President Barack Obama commuted her sentence to a total of seven years dating from her arrest in 2010.

KEY PLAYER

EDWARD SNOWDEN
A former CIA employee, Edward Snowden rose to prominence in the public eye when, during his time as a contractor for the National Security Agency (NSA), he leaked over a million classified U.S. government documents to journalists. In June 2013, the U.S. Department of Justice charged him with espionage and theft of government property. He subsequently fled to Russia, where he currently has been given asylum until 2020. Snowden has claimed that he leaked the classified documents because he felt their contents were unconstitutional, and that he had become disillusioned with his government. As he has become a subject of much-heated debate in security circles and the media, Snowden has been hailed as a hero and a patriot by some, and reviled as a dissident and traitor by others.

STEALING FROM THE NSA The first question one might well ask when looking at the case of Edward Snowden is, why was it so easy for him to steal info? Well, it wasn't exactly "easy," but it wasn't as hard as it would have been in another era. Thinking about the key concept of confidentiality, and how difficult it is to implement it, things get harder at the level of systems administrator—someone entrusted to have access to a lot of systems for the purpose of making it work in the desired fashion.

The hardest thing to do on a network is classify data. Humans tend to overclassify data, and it's particularly difficult to classify the information that is already on the network after it's there (*ex post facto* classification), as opposed to classification of data that is being newly created.

The Human Factor In an intelligence agency, we begin with the premise that everything within its walls is already important enough to be secret—the fact that they collect it at all speaks to its importance. But even if that weren't true, even if Snowden worked at, say, an insurance company, where each and every fact had been accurately classified, the issue would have been the same: He still would have needed to be able to poke around the systems and ensure that all the whatsits were in the right place. That's because he was a systems administrator with administrative access, also known as super-user access. Typically, by the time you get to be a network administrator on a network that carries classified information, you've been checked out pretty thoroughly, passed lots of tests—including polygraph examinations in which you're quizzed about your lifestyle—and generally thought to be "squared away."

I spoke with a former systems administrator with Top Secret/Secure Compartmentalized Information (TS/SCI) clearance about this. The system Snowden stole from is at the highest classification level. In order to get access to the system, one would have to have the TS/SCI background check and the lifestyle polygraph mentioned above. As we said, Snowden was a systems administrator, so by the nature of his job, he would have had extensive access across the network; getting access to the data was fairly trivial for him at that point.

Getting the Goods The actual difficulty would have been getting the data out of the building. On TS/SCI systems, all removable media capabilities (like USB, CD, and DVD) are disabled, so there is no means for regular people to get information off the systems. There is an exception, though, for systems administrators. Within a sysadmin shop, there are typically one or two systems that have the ability to write CDs or take a USB drive. Sometimes, there are completely legitimate reasons why one would have to transport data between non-networked systems. For Snowden, the theft was not rocket science but a matter of abusing his trusted position.

Two things could have been implemented but weren't (and probably are now) to stop this: better internal data segmentation and two-person integrity controls (TPI) for systems administrators who want to use removable media—think of nuclear keys and you get the idea. It's a pain in the ass and it's inelegant, but it does work.

The fact is, getting that kind of access, despite how easy it may have looked, wasn't easy. It may have taken him five minutes to steal the data, but it took him years to know which data to steal and to be placed in the position that enabled him to steal it.

GOOD TO KNOW

BAD PRACTICE It's easy to look at the glamorous, freedom-loving aspect of whistleblowing without seeing the potential dark side or unintended consequences. In addition to facts and figures, Snowden's leaked documents also revealed the methods and capabilities of programs used by multiple governments to monitor covert communications on the internet—including methods to monitor those involved in human trafficking. Once these programs were revealed, these kidnapping, slaving criminals changed their tactics, forcing international law enforcement to find new ways to intercept and decode these transmissions. On that basis, forgive me if I don't refer to Snowden as a hero.

KEY CONCEPT

BLOWING A WHISTLE
Not all informants are created equally. A "whistleblower" and a "leaker" are actually two separate types of individuals. In the case of the former, these are typically dutiful people who happen to discover something that is illegal or unethical, and then try to report the problem through the proper internal mechanisms; when they fail or are unable to do so (there can be a variety of reasons for failing), they report the wrongdoing to an external source but limit their reporting to only what has gone wrong. A leaker, meanwhile, can be considered someone who, whether out of carelessness or a desire to seek fame, avoids or ignores the standard channels followed by a whistleblower and instead disseminates the information in a less-conscientious fashion, without making much effort to do so discretely or with regard to the repercussions.

KEY PLAYER

JULIAN ASSANGE AND WIKILEAKS Australian-born journalist and publisher Julian Assange is the cocreator and director of WikiLeaks, which publishes leaked sensitive documents. WikiLeaks has existed since 2006 but came into prominence as a result of the documents leaked by Chelsea Manning. By 2015, WikiLeaks had published more than ten million of what Assange describes as "the world's most persecuted documents." As with other key players, Assange has been called a hero, traitor, and opportunist. In 2010, Assange visited Sweden, where he became the subject of sexual assault allegations. He was allowed to leave, but later Sweden asked for him to be extradited. He has spent the last several years living in the Ecuadorian embassy in London. In 2017, WikiLeaks published a trove of CIA hacking documents said to be the largest ever.

WHY AND HOW INFORMATION GETS OUT One key difference between a Daniel Ellsberg, an Edward Snowden, and a Julian Assange is that Snowden and the like are individual actors, whereas Assange's WikiLeaks is a clearinghouse—a brokerage of information, if you will. And thus, their methods, their motives, and their reception by media and security experts vary.

Snowden's Motivation As an individual operator, Snowden's claims as to why he did what he did are quite divisive. One side sees a freedom fighter: a man truly dedicated to the idea that his government had run amok, conducting mass surveillance of literally every adult in the United States and Europe through extensive monitoring of a wide range of technologies. To this group, giving up his six-figure income and an arguably cushy life in Hawaii for a one-bedroom flat near the Maryina Roshcha District is further proof of Snowden's dedication to these fundamental propositions.

The other side sees agencies working to capture legitimate signals intelligence of the sort that has been their remit since SIGINT was the lynchpin on which the Allies achieved victory in World War II. This intelligence is a well-defined and anonymized mass collection of information that is freely available: call data records of numbers and call metadata inside the United States, and call record and content outside the United States joined only with properly defined and legally sanctioned oversight. Along with traditional signals targets, this intel is sought by every country on Earth for the same reason: the protection of life.

Your personal beliefs about Snowden probably depend a lot on what you do for a living, whether you've served in the military, and your general political stance. And the "truth" probably lies in the middle. From what we have seen, there appear to have been some terrible abuses in the U.S. system of checks and balances, especially when it comes to the Foreign Intelligence Surveillance Act of 1978 and its court. Many of the programs were described to the world by journalists who admittedly knew nothing of intelligence, surveillance, or even encryption before Snowden quite literally dropped the materials into their hands (saying, cynically, that as journalists they would know best how to release the information).

Assange and the Profit Motive Where Snowden might claim to be inspired by Ellsberg, Assange sought to influence and provoke leaks by people like Chelsea Manning. In that sense, Assange's WikiLeaks behaves in a manner that is similar to an intelligence service: Assange and his associates act as officers, who seek agents in various positions of authority in governmental office to provide them with intelligence. The agents may turn over the intelligence for a range of reasons that they believe justify their actions, which may be anything from misplaced patriotism to revenge to idealism (WikiLeaks is not known to pay for leaks).

Depending on your viewpoint, this may be "better" or "worse" than traditional espionage, but espionage it is. Chelsea Manning's turning over of the documents that would ultimately make up the trove of diplomatic cables released by WikiLeaks presented the United States with a situation in which the entire world became privy in one fell swoop to the most intimate minutiae of its diplomatic communications—petty, trivial, damning, controversial, telling . . . It was an intelligence bonanza for any nation intent on understanding how the United States does this kind of thing.

GOOD TO KNOW

THE TOP THREE LEAKS Here are the most interesting, extensive, or devastating leaks in the history of modern intelligence breaches.

LEAK	YEAR	NATURE OF LEAK
PENTAGON PAPERS	1971	Daniel Ellsberg, then a U.S. military analyst, released documents to the *New York Times*, detailing more than twenty years of the government's involvement in Vietnam.
EDWARD SNOWDEN	2013	Leaked over a million documents relating to U.S. security policies and practices.
OFFICE OF PERSONNEL MANAGEMENT	2015	The United States Office of Personnel Management announced that 21.5 million records had been breached, consisting of all the personnel files on applicants for national security clearance.

KEY PLAYER

THOMAS DRAKE An NSA employee, Drake worked on "Trailblazer," a $1.2 billion USD data-mining program he felt intruded on civil rights and national treasure. After years of trying to report internally, he went public. He was arrested in 2010 and charged aggressively with willful retention of national defense information, obstructing justice, and making false statements. Drake spent much of the time awaiting trial (he refused to admit wrongdoing or to plea-bargain) working as a Genius at an Apple store. The government dropped all charges, in return for a guilty plea to misuse of an agency computer. The judge howled that the government mishandled the entire affair, saying it had destroyed Drake's career, taken his salary, and his pension. Drake got a year of probation and community service. Today, Drake is looked upon by many in the government as a genuine (if misguided and wrong) "whistleblower."

KEY PLAYER

INTELLIGENCE AND DATA COLLECTION
For all the glamour that spy movies give it, intelligence is simply data that has been collected and then analyzed for a purpose. There's certain intelligence in both WikiLeaks and in the stolen Snowden documents from which a foreign intelligence service can deduce or otherwise conclude our sources and methods. By giving adversaries insight into these, Snowden allowed them to close pathways of information collection. If they can conclude the sources, the sources are endangered. Arguably, others must presumably be placed at risk in order to establish new means of collections.

WHY IS IT SO HARD TO PROTECT INFORMATION?
Data classification is highly complex, and because it is contextual, machines just aren't any good at it. The classic example of AOL locking people out of a breast cancer support group because AOL technicians tried to block the word "breast" may or may not be true, but it's certainly a good example of the difficulty faced by machines trying to discern the nuance of words in context. Even for humans, the process is difficult, because the context even of certain phrases can raise issues.

Technical Issues Data theft technology, which is referred to by the industry as data loss prevention (DLP), is fairly complex, but it's still very rudimentary in terms of intelligence. DLP is best at strings of defined lengths—credit card, social security, and account numbers are easiest to detect. But even within those, we have tremendous variation. For example, consider how you write phone numbers: 888/235-1212; 888-235-1212; 888.235.1212; (888)235-1212; (888) 235-1212; 888) 235-1212. These are all ways of writing the same thing. Now do it with words. How to compare all these variants in real time, as someone's trying to send an email and you're trying to scan it and determine whether the email contains something sensitive before the email goes out the door? Well, the trick is to buffer everything, truncate and stem all the words and phrases, remove all the extraneous characters, then hash everything, then compare hashes. It's faster. This can be done in an amazingly small amount of time. But it's still nowhere near foolproof; what if the file is encrypted?

The Enemy Within What if, as we've just discussed, the data thief is your system administrator? The fact is, catching data thieves is very hard unless you've classified it all very well in advance, limited access to it, removed the removable media options, and limited the ways to get data off your network. For most companies, that's not commercially feasible.

Bottom line? Data classification is very difficult. Businesses should pay close attention to how they classify and provide access to important data, and how people can get access to it. And data theft is incredibly hard to stop.

THE TAKEAWAY

What does government security and international espionage have to do with you? The lessons learned here are more helpful than you might think.

BASIC SECURITY	• Classify your data in two categories: public and private. Make sure to keep those records separate! • Treat employees well. This is always a good idea, but particularly relevant if potentially disgruntled workers have access to classified information.
ADVANCED MEASURES	• Encrypt your private data whenever you email it and wherever you store it. And be incredibly careful about who has the keys. • Destroy all data you don't need, regularly.
TINFOIL-HAT BRIGADE	• Use DLP software to detect data leaving your business. • Go beyond the basics and classify documents and emails to understand when sensitive information may be leaving your network, and then speak with or take punitive action against employees who break your policies.

*

IF YOU SHOULD HAPPEN TO FIND YOURSELF IN A WHISTLE-BLOWING SITUATION, REVIEW YOUR LEGAL RIGHTS AND THE PROPER CHANNELS FOR REPORTING THE ISSUE TO AVOID BECOMING A LEAKER.

INTERNATIONAL CYBERSECURITY

THE DANGER OF A FOREIGN GOVERNMENTS LAUNCHING A CYBER ATTACK HAS BEEN A SECURITY ISSUE FOR SOME TIME, BUT NOT UNTIL 2016 WHEN RUSSIA HACKED THE AMERICAN PRESIDENTIAL ELECTION DID IT HIT THE FRONT PAGES.

We close this book by taking a look at cybersecurity on a global scale. Know who's already doing that? Every government on Earth, and each has been at it for a very long time. Nation-states consider "cyber" to be a key area of operations. It's where they communicate, spy, command, and control—and sometimes, where they attack.

Cyberspying against the United States became so problematic by 2011 that the military changed its policy on cyberattacks to "equivalency"—essentially, online attacks are now viewed just like physical ones. An unnamed military source told the *Wall Street Journal* that "If you shut down our power grid, maybe we will put a missile down one of your smokestacks." It was as a clear warning to Chinese and Russian hackers, the latter of whom had recently used cyber attacks to turn off the lights in Estonia, and then again in Georgia, as precursors to invasion.

Nations have a number of ways to rattle their cyber sabers. At the low end of aggression is intellectual-property theft and piracy. At the high end is the notion of crashing another nation's infrastructure or hacking its military. And what about non-nation-states doing such things? Could a teenage hacker really start a world war?

CUCKOO FOR CYBER SPIES Although cyberterrorism has been fairly big news as of late, it's actually far from a new concept. The contemporary cyber espionage era started up pretty much as soon as computers were first connected to public networks. For a real thriller of a hacker story, try reading Clifford Stoll's 1989 classic *The Cuckoo's Egg*. This nonfiction page-turner tells the incredible but true-to-life tale of how a systems administrator doggedly chased down a 75-cent UNIX-system accounting error, which unfolded into ultimately taking down a complex, KGB-funded cyber operation in 1986 that was seeking to steal U.S. military secrets through the fledgling internet. Stoll solved the case himself in spite of a series of infuriatingly dense FBI agents straight out of Central Casting, along with a cast of dozens of square-jawed spooks, each one of them more impossibly unhelpful than the last.

KEY CONCEPT

TRADE SECRETS
Intellectual property, or IP, is how businesses turn ideas into money—maybe a new fabrication process or the ingredients that make up their secret sauce. Here are key things companies keep in their IP portfolios.

Business Processes A closely guarded list of materials used to make products.

Bill of Materials A list used to make products, and closely guarded by manufacturers.

Software Firmware and apps are included. This is the core of many firms' IP portfolios and what makes a hunk of plastic into a beloved consumer electronic device.

Road Map The list of product features and functions that a company plans to introduce.

R&D The research and development of new products and features.

STEALING OUR GOOD STUFF So, what is intellectual property (IP) anyway? The legal definition is "creations of the mind, such as inventions; literary and artistic works; designs; and symbols, names, and images used in commerce." The term covers everything from art and music to apps and code. Theft of IP isn't super glamorous, so most cases, even multibillion-dollar ones, don't make the news outside of the business pages. The U.S. government recently estimated that cybertheft of intellectual property costs the economy $300 billion USD a year. If you find yourself wondering why cyber espionage is so prevalent, it's simple: It is substantially cheaper and faster to steal stuff than it is to build it from scratch.

"The only adversary one needs to worry about," says David Etue, from cyber security firm Rapid7, "is the one who figures out that he can steal for $2 million what it takes you $2 billion to research and develop." Etue is right. It's much easier for foreign government-controlled companies to simply steal their way to success than it is to build it through R&D.

Industrial Espionage It's not just commercial IP that gets ripped off. Drug trials, oil and fuel formulations, and other industrial secrets are in great demand. And it's not just the Chinese and the Russians doing the dirty work. Industrial espionage is top of the pops in France, as well as in many other nations. What a lot of people may not realize is that, to China and Russia, commercial adversaries count as targets for government espionage. Chinese and Russian companies are often owned by the government, so interference

THE COST OF CYBER THEFT
The thing about IP is that it frequently forms the core of a company's identity. A stolen computer can be replaced, stolen money can be recouped. A cyber breach of this kind is more like identity theft on a grand scale, and the real and intangible costs can be staggering.

VISIBLE COSTS OF IP THEFT
- Investigations
- Need to Notify Customers
- Monitoring Customer Security Post-Breach
- Regulatory Compliance Issues
- PR to Combat Negative Publicity
- Upgrade Cyber Security & Training
- Lawyers' Fees, Other Legal Costs

HIDDEN COSTS OF IP THEFT
- High Insurance Premiums
- Lower Credit Rating
- Lost Productivity & Low Morale
- Lost Customers
- Loss of Potential Future Business
- Reputation and Value of Brand Suffer
- R&D Time and Investment Wasted

from government or military hacking groups against American competitors is seen not a business chicanery but a matter of national security. It's not about the money, per se. It's about securing the future—especially in the realms of critical infrastructure, energy, medicine, and finance. It's business as usual.

National Security That's why, when the United States began shouting its protestations about Russian involvement in the 2016 hack of the Democratic National Committee, none other than Shawn Henry—the former assistant executive director of the FBI, for which he had largely established its cyber practice, and the man who led the investigation into the DNC hack for CrowdStrike—spoke out in the press about it in no uncertain terms: "It's the job of every foreign intelligence service to collect intelligence against their adversaries," he told the *Washington Post*. For the Chinese and Russians, commercial secrets and commercial organizations are considered legitimate nation-state adversaries.

CASE STUDY

HOW THEFT HURTS BUSINESS The poster child for nation-state intellectual property theft was American Superconductor Corp (AMSC) doing business with its Chinese partner, Sinovel Wind Group. AMSC made the software that drove Sinovel's turbines, and everything was just ducky until an AMSC engineer was on a Sinovel turbine one day and noticed that the firmware was, well, different. In fact, Sinovel had completely replaced the AMSC firmware with its own version, based on IP it had stolen from AMSC. Thus began the best-known case in the United States of theft by a Chinese company of an American firm's intellectual property. AMSC says it lost $1.2 billion USD, because Sinovel accounted for 80 percent of AMSC's revenues (making this case an object lesson on customer diversity as well as Chinese hacking).

You might ask why you should care if some random company gets ripped off. Simple answer: Who do you think they're going to pass those costs down to? Yep, the old end-user, a.k.a. you.

SECURITY BASIC

BORDER SECURITY A relatively new concern in 2017 was searches of electronic devices by U.S. Customs and Border Protection. The law allows these searches, but they are still rare—in 2016, there were 390 million crossings and 24,000 searches. Still, if you don't want Uncle Sam plowing through your hard drive, power down devices fully before crossing borders (cold boot security is often stronger than when merely suspended or locked) and minimize the amount and sensitivity of data and equipment you transport across borders. Be aware that citizens cannot be denied entry but can be detained briefly for questioning. Under no circumstances should you lie to CBP officials. If they request or demand a password, it is your right to refuse to comply, but equipment can still be detained for weeks or months. If this happens, you should consider legal assistance.
—Ryan Lackey, Founder, Reset Security

KEY CONCEPT

ZERO-DAY Security researchers seek out vulnerabilities in code. When they find one, they have several courses of action. If they work for a government spy agency or a criminal gang, they may choose to create code that can exploit the vulnerability they have found—this weaponized code, before it is disclosed to anyone else, is called a "zero-day." It comes from the amount of time, in days, once the vulnerability is known until the maker of the software can fix the problem. On day zero (which is actually the first day—as computers always count everything starting from zero), the weapon is active. The ethics of selling zero-days is debatable. Companies that sell them to governments argue that, so long as the transaction is legal, the ethics are beside the point. Critics say that governments can use zero-days to attack and monitor dissidents. It's a tough call.

INFRASTRUCTURE ATTACKS In March of 2007, researchers at Idaho National Laboratory sent a test cyberattack to breakers that protected a 2.25-megawatt diesel-powered generator. Within a minute, the generator, weighing tons, literally jumped in the air, began to smoke, and was destroyed. Official video of this attack—considered the first public demonstration of a successful cyberattack on critical infrastructure—was leaked to CNN. The "Aurora Vulnerability," as it was called, was shocking for its simplicity, and cyber security experts began pointing out that America's supervisory control and data acquisition (SCADA) networks and industrial control system (ICS) networks are aged, fragile, overwhelmingly small, and privately owned—so this problem is not something that the U.S. government can simply order fixed. Ultimately, if a local power department decides not to invest $3,000 USD in patch management, that's a private business decision that the government can't overrule, absent clear threat and a court order.

The media became fascinated by attacks on SCADA and ICS, seeing every shutdown as a potential hack. Several attacks on critical infrastructure have happened, and each has been denied vocally by some. In 2009, widespread power outages in Brazil were reportedly caused by hackers; experts reported that it was soot, not hackers. Senior U.S. officials countered "nuh-uh," and it's never been settled.

Russian Aggressions No such uncertainty exists when it comes to Russian tactics: Russian government-mounted cyber attacks in the form of website takedowns, DNS attacks, and ultimately the complete blackout of Georgian internet traffic, which served as a precursor to invasion in 2008. This tactic has become a standard by Russia, which rather openly cyber-attacked the Ukrainian power grid in 2016, shutting down more than fifty power substations.

ATTACK DISTRIBUTION

No matter the time of year, criminals, activists, and others are busy with cyber attacks and other operations.

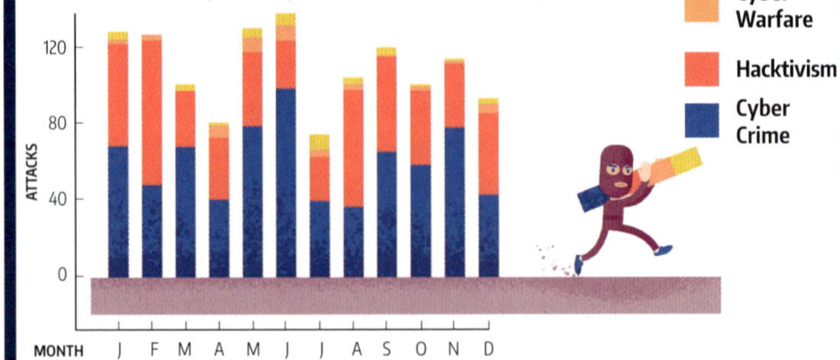

What's at Risk? The scary news is that the SCADA systems in control of the nation's power are no any worse off than the systems that protect water, sewage, or other critical infrastructure, such as oil and gas. The good news is that, over the past few years, the federal government, along with the North American Electric Reliability Corporation and other groups, has been focusing intensely on SCADA and ICS issues. The problems are not yet solved, but we are in marginally more aware than we were a few years ago. That said, attacks have indeed been weaponized, and more things are connected to the internet than ever before (even though they shouldn't be), so it all may be a wash.

GOOD TO KNOW

PAGING YOUR INFRASTRUCTURE Does anyone use pagers anymore? Funny thing—apparently, a large number of critical infrastructure players, including chemical manufacturers, nuclear and electric plants, defense contractors, and others rely on unsecured wireless pagers to automate their industrial control systems. According to a 2016 report, this practice opens them to malicious hacks and espionage. In the report, researchers from security firm Trend Micro collected more than fifty-four million pages during a four-month span using low-cost hardware. In some cases, the messages alerted recipients to unsafe conditions affecting mission-critical infrastructure as they were detected. According to the report, "These unencrypted pager messages are a valuable source of passive intelligence, the gathering of information that is unintentionally leaked by networked or connected organizations. . . . Taken together, threat actors can do heavy reconnaissance on targets by making sense of the acquired information through paging messages. Though we are not well versed with the terms and information used in some of the sectors in our research, we were able to determine what the pages mean, including how attackers would make use of them in an elaborate targeted attack or how industry competitors would take advantage of such information."

T/F

AMERICA'S NUCLEAR LAUNCH CODES ARE KEPT ON FLOPPIES

TRUE Currently, if you want to launch a nuclear strike, you need technology from the 1970s in order to do so—an 8-inch floppy disk of the kind most modern adults have never even seen. It's not unreasonable to assume that this is on purpose—sort of a *Battlestar Galactica* scenario, where our most sensitive data is kept in such a way that our enemies (or teenage hackers) can't get at it. In fact, the truth is much more mundane—the U.S. government's cyber systems are woefully out of date, and we spend some $60 billion USD annually on maintaining those outdated systems.

IF YOU TRAVEL ABROAD, FAMILIARIZE YOURSELF WITH LOCAL CYBER SECURITY LAWS, AVOID PUBLIC WI-FI IF AT ALL POSSIBLE, AND PROTECT YOUR DEVICES TO THE FULLEST EXTENT THAT YOU CAN, PHYSICALLY AND DIGITALLY.

MOBILE PHONE HACKS From sometime before 2004 (during the run up to the Olympic games in Greece) until January of 2005, either a criminal-based or nation-state-sponsored hacking gang engaged in a mass mobile phone network hacking operation. This group was tapping into Vodafone's switches in Greece, and targeting a range of calls to specific phones. Targets of this hacking incident included the mobile phones belonging to ministers of Greek national defense, foreign affairs, and justice departments; the mayor of Athens; the European Union commissioner for Greece; a variety of individuals engaged in civil rights, anti-globalization, and peace activism; and diplomats carrying mobile phones belonging to the U.S. embassy at Athens. Since that time, security experts have pointed out similar cases around the world in which the mobile networks in various countries have been compromised.

A History of Vulnerability None of these issues are particularly new—mobile networks, just like any other network, are susceptible to security issues. Nonetheless, occasionally this sort of thing becomes big news. In 2016, we learned of vulnerabilities in a digital signaling protocol that mobile phone carriers such as AT&T, T-Mobile, and Sprint use to track their users' identity, location, and more. A *60 Minutes* segment highlighted a hacker using that vulnerability to access phone data. That episode scared the pants off of seemingly everyone who saw it—and a bunch who just heard about it second-hand. Mobile networks are being patched as fast as they can, but SS7 (Signaling System No. 7, a common network protocol for handling phone calls and SMS messages) is only one of many vulnerabilities in how mobile operators handle the complex task of routing more and more voice and data calls each day.

MOBILE PRIVACY

Your mobile device's signal and data could be intercepted mid-transmission, and you might never know it.

Mobile Privacy Today During the past handful of years, the privacy community has begun to seriously question how good law enforcement really is at intercepting cellular signals and harvesting mobile phone data. The equipment for doing this sort of thing has been available to federal agencies and to some larger law enforcement agencies for several years by now. Technical advances have brought the costs down, while increased reliance on smartphones by individuals has increased the bang for the buck these products can provide, so more agencies are using them. These include tools called IMSI-catchers, which we've discussed briefly earlier in this book. IMSI stands for "international mobile subscriber identity"—that is, the unique identification number tagged to each mobile phone, which then allows a cellular network to distinguish each user from another. This device works as a man-in-the-middle platform for eavesdropping on phones on the GSM (global system for mobile) network.

Essentially, IMSI-catchers are portable base stations that can simulate a powerful cellular phone signal tower so that your phone, which always seeks out the most powerful signal within range, associates itself with it. Once that happens, the IMSI-catcher will intercept your signal before passing it on to a real tower (so that your call still does go through), but it captures everything that both sides say all the while—and you probably won't even notice.

Spying on the Airwaves Think IMSI-catchers are the thing you need to worry about if you want to avoid being eavesdropped on? Unfortunately, that's far from the case. The emergence of 4G LTE (long-term evolution) networking, also known as LTE, addressed some of these privacy issues, but, in 2015 researchers released information about kits that run about $1,200 USD and allow anyone who has a laptop and a universal radio software peripheral (USRP) and the proper software to intercept and locate 4G LTE traffic.

Another thing to consider is the advent of open platforms for mobile telephone operators. What Linux is to operating systems such as OpenBTS and OpenLTE are to mobile telephony: a set of freely available tools that can enable highly sophisticated mobile operations. David Burgess, one of the creators of OpenBTS, set up a mobile network at the Burning Man festival using his OpenBTS platform—and it worked just fine for everyone using it. As these tools to interact with increasingly smarter phones become less expensive and more commonly available, and as we rely more on our mobile devices for everything, we can expect even more attacks on cellular phones and mobile networks using this vector.

KILLER APP

BURN, BABY, BURN
A number of apps out there let you create a new, anonymous, and theoretically untraceable phone number that you can use from your mobile. These are helpful even if you're not engaging in international espionage. They're great for talking to potential dates, selling things on Craigslist, or in a dangerous situation where someone like an abusive spouse or parent is monitoring your calls. Here are some popular options:

Burner One of the best and easiest-to-use apps, but it only works in the United States and Canada.

Hushed Works in forty countries over VoIP, so it will cut into your data plan if you use your cellular internet connection.

CoverMe This app has numbers that appear to originate from the United States, Canada, UK, China, and Mexico.

ON A TRIP OUTSIDE THE COUNTRY, CONSIDER RENTING A LOCAL MOBILE PHONE OR COMPUTER TO AVOID ANY CUSTOMS ISSUES OR SEARCHING OF YOUR DEVICES UPON RETURN.

WHAT'S THE BUZZ? After 9/11, one of the most commonly heard terms from the intelligence community in the public domain was "chatter." It's a brilliant term because it sounds highly specific, but it's really quite generic, encompassing signals intelligence and publicly overheard sentiment on radio, television, internet forums and chatrooms, newspaper editorials, and gossip. Basically, chatter can mean just about anything.

We won't hear anything useful about SIGINT being gathered today (unless it's being proffered as a justification for military actions or economic sanctions), because our intelligence agencies focusing on that (mainly the National Security Agency) are incredibly good at not saying things. But we do understand from a few peeks inside how chatter is used by professionals to track terror groups.

Taking Responsibility If 9/11 resulted from a breakdown of intelligence upon a national scale, at the New York Police Department it was seen as a failure to take responsibility for the city's destiny. New York doesn't stay on the wrong side of a problem very long; at about 9 a.m. on September 11, 2001, senior officials at the NYPD surveyed the smoldering wreckage of the World Trade Center and said, "Yeah, this is not going to happen ever again." They began to create an intelligence capability that has become an extraordinary agency in its own right, combining tradecraft and procedures imported from agencies like the CIA (David Cohen, the NYPD's first commissioner for intelligence, is ex-CIA) and a hodgepodge of methods that other agencies practiced. The result was uniquely New York, because the NYPD got to do something few ever get to do: start from scratch and create a culture.

Doing It Right Like many other intelligence agencies, the NYPD created a group of incredibly capable young officers to be stationed around the world to provide continuous, on-the-ground intelligence. And one thing that the NYPD Intelligence Bureau had done very well was to establish it early on. Uniquely, for its cyber capability, the bureau used NYPD detectives to focus on looking for threats, capabilities, and intent, while also relying on civilian analysts to provide the language expertise (everything from Arabic to Pashto to Urdu) and for their cyber-fu. Meanwhile, the bureau also allowed the detective-investigators to remain professionals in their highly significant areas of expertise.

Typically, the IB Cyber Unit focuses on detection and investigation of radicalization and various threats as they pertain to New York City. In a nutshell, the team focuses on the enormous pile of people saying stuff that sounds radical, separating out people who are just spouting off or exercising free speech from those truly thinking about radicalization, then investigating and separating the curious from those with true intent.

WHO'S BEING ATTACKED?

As one might expect, the vast majority of cyberattacks are launched at the USA, but many other nations fall victim as well.

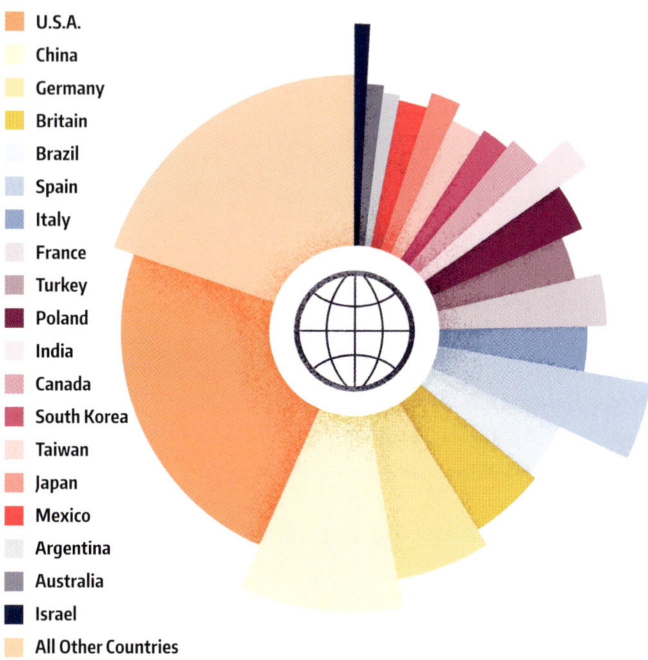

SECURITY BASIC

YOU ARE FOR SALE In 2017, the U.S. Congress approved measures to roll back privacy laws, allowing ISPs to access and sell data about their consumers' browsing histories to advertisers and other third parties. This means that there will be more general access to the specifics of every darn page that you visit (yep, even those ones) than ever before. Because of this, using your own domain name server and anonymizing traffic is very important. We recommend using a browser such as Tor, correctly configured, or a trusted virtual private network client; encrypted DNS service such as the one offered by OpenDNS; the HTTPS Everywhere plug-in; and an anonymous search engine, like DuckDuckGo or StartPage, to protect the privacy of what you view on the internet. It's not that you have something to hide but a simple matter of basic personal liberty.

ONE SILVER LINING TO THINK OF REGARDING CYBER WAR . . . AT LEAST IT'S EASIER TO REBOOT A NETWORK THAN REBUILD A CITY.

CYBER TERRORISM In the last five years, many of the cyber-attack tools that were once used exclusively by nation-states have become more easy to obtain, meaning that they can now also be used by criminal gangs and—at least in theory—terror groups as well. But buying a great piano really cheap doesn't mean you can suddenly play Chopin. The money and training that go in to a cyber operation is the true barrier to entry.

During the 2016 election, hacking by Russia caused tremendous disruption in the United States. We now know that during the six- to nine-month gestation period after the Russians gained entry to the network of the Democratic National Committee, but before they began to release email publicly, their activities consisted mainly of lateral movement within the network. During that time, the attackers engaged in rather routine but essential activities of a long-term network reconnaissance operation, including data classification and location. The hackers were answering the questions: What does the DNC have? Where do they keep it? How do they use it? How do they access it? Basically, they were learning the answer to "What does 'normal' look like in this organization?" All this showed one important difference between a nation-state attack and those mounted by terror groups: tradecraft.

Art and Craft Tradecraft is the techniques, methods, and tools that together form the art of spying, and it's not something that comes easily. It takes years of experience, lots of money, and great leadership and training. Mostly, when we look at terror groups, we see them spending what money and leadership and training resources they have not on tradecraft but on materiel and logistics for attack: moving men, guns, and bombs across distances; getting them training; smuggling them across borders; and mounting attacks.

Hackers Are Everywhere The barriers terrorists being able to launch a cyber attack are getting lower. When we look at the troubles that groups like Anonymous and LulzSec have caused law enforcement and other government groups, the disruption was significant. Their success was based on a commonly agreed-upon mission, a decentralized command and control, and the availability of free, easy-to-use, and easy-to-learn hacking and attack tools. This sounds like the basis of a classic terrorist attack, and it can be used by groups such as ISIS once the cyberweaponry they would need has be simplified to the point that it's easily adopted by groups with minimal resources. It just takes a small group of radicalized, computer-literate believers to tip these scales.

THE TAKEAWAY

Protecting your data when you travel is fairly easy. Stopping a global cyber war—not so much. Still, there are always ways to be prepared.

BASIC SECURITY	• Protect your IP online and when traveling. • Encrypt all products and IP-related communications.
ADVANCED MEASURES	• Use purpose-built devices for cross-border travel. • Maintain minimal mobile mail settings (no one needs more than thirty days of email on their phone at this point). • Encrypt everything. • Minimize data sets provided to business partners. • Audit partners' security as you would your own.
TINFOIL-HAT BRIGADE	• Prepare for an infrastructure attack. • Get off the electric grid with solar power. • Prepare to have an interruption in your water supply. • Practice self-sufficiency.

TRUE STORY

SHALL WE PLAY A GAME? In 1983, a movie called *WarGames* captured the world's imagination with the plotline in which a teenage hacker almost starts World War III when he hacks into a Defense Department computer. One major unexpected consequence of that film was that then-president Ronald Reagan saw it and was subsequently moved to devote resources into what we now call cyber security. A great number of young hackers were also inspired by the movie, perhaps most the famous being a group of Milwaukee-area high-school students who went by the collective name The 414s (for their area code in Wisconsin). The 414s breached a number of big corporate networks for fun, simply as a prank rather than to steal or damage anything. Since hacking was more difficult to prosecute at the time, they were finally charged with making illegal phone calls.

GLOSSARY

Credentials A document or certificate proving a person's identity or qualifications.

Encryption The process of converting information or data into a code, especially to prevent unauthorized access.

Entrepreneur One who organizes, manages, and assumes the risks of a business or enterprise.

Expenditure The action of spending funds, or an amount of money spent.

Firewall A part of a computer system that is designed to block unauthorized access.

Fraud Deceit or trickery.

Hacking To gain illegal access to a computer network or system.

Hijack To illegally seize something.

Illicit Forbidden by law or rules.

Infrastructure The basic physical and organizational structures needed for the operation of something.

Malware Software designed to interfere with a computer's normal functioning.

Manipulate To change something by unfair means to serve one's purpose.

Monetize To coin into money or establish as legal tender.

Phishing A scam by which an Internet user is duped into revealing personal or confidential information which the scammer can use illicitly.

Ransomware A type of malicious software designed to block access to a computer system until a sum of money is paid.

Revenue The total income produced by a given source.

Software Something used or associated with hardware, such as programs for a computer.

Surveillance Close watch kept over someone or something.

Vector A line that is defined by its start and end point.

Virtual Being on or simulated on a computer or computer network.

FOR FURTHER READING

Flores, Maria Antonieta. *The Language of Cybersecurity.* Laguna Hills: XML Press, 2018.

Kosseff, Jeff. *Cybersecurity Law.* Hoboken: Wiley, 2017.

Meeuwisse, Raef. *Cybersecurity for Beginners.* London, UK: Cyber Simplicity Ltd, 2017.

Meeuwisse, Raef. *Cybersecurity: Home and Small Business.* London, UK: Cyber Simplicity Ltd, 2016.

Singer, P.W., and Allan Friedman. *Cybersecurity and Cyberwar: What Everyone Needs to Know.* Oxford, UK: Oxford University Press, 2014.

FOR MORE INFORMATION

Be Ready, Be Informed

https://www.ready.gov/cybersecurity

Understand the fundamental concepts of cybersecurity and how to use them.

Homeland Security

https://www.dhs.gov/topic/cybersecurity

Learn about the cybersecurity strategies employed by the Department of Homeland Security.

Introduction to Cybersecurity

http://www.umuc.edu/academic-programs/cyber-security/about.cfm

Discover cybersecurity career opportunities and more.

What You Need to Know

https://www.forbes.com/sites/laurencebradford/2018/03/30/why-people-should-learn-about-cybersecurity-in-2018/#171136325d00

An informative article about how technology affects modern life.

INDEX

INDEX